How can today's churches and their members work together in harmonious unity within denominations, and in transdenominational associations, in an age which is characterized by independence, dissonance, and self-assertiveness?

In this seminal volume internationally-known practical theologian and social psychologist, Craig Skinner, confronts such critical concerns from fresh and challenging perspectives.

He explores the spiritual, family, and behavioral ties which bind believers together as well as the doctrinal one. He affirms that a biblical foundation exists for a healing theology of Baptist unity within the neglected dynamics of attitude, insight, focus, and conduct.

Thoroughly faithful to the New Testament this study (geared for a wide range of lay persons as well as for professionals in all evangelical churches) is written in straight forward and clearly communicated language centering around Ephesians chapter four. It offers constructive therapy as well as a clear diagnosis of many present ills, and highlights some innovative avenues for relief which appear to be largely overlooked amid current stresses.

As a contemporary exposition of true Christian unity this study supplies a fresh biblical theology applicable for all who confess Jesus Christ as Lord. Laypersons and professional Southern Baptist leaders, from any part of the political or theological spectrum, (whose Sunday School Board, and Women's Missionary Union have recently enlarged their vision to include the supply of resources to other evangelicals) will find this material to be especially valuable and relevant.

TIES THAT BIND

MAINSTREAM FOUNDATIONS FOR A HEALING THEOLOGY OF BAPTIST UNITY

TIES
THAT
BIND

MAINSTREAM FOUNDATIONS
FOR A HEALING THEOLOGY
OF BAPTIST UNITY

CRAIG SKINNER

FOREWORD BY:

DR. JOHN NEWPORT
FORMER PROVOST AND V.P. ACADEMIC AFFAIRS
SOUTHWESTERN BAPTIST THEOLOGICAL SEMINARY

CHRISTIAN UNIVERSITIES PRESS
SAN FRANCISCO

published by

CHRISTIAN UNIVERSITIES PRESS
P.O. Box 2590
San Francisco, CA 94133

Design and Typesetting by Diane Spencer Hume

Library of Congress Cataloging-in-Publication Data

Skinner, Craig.
    Ties that bind : mainstream foundations for a healing theology of
Baptist unity / Craig Skinner.
        p. cm.
    Includes bibliographical references.
    ISBN 9-883255-08-2:$24.95. -- ISBN 1-88-883255-01-5 (pbk.) : $12.95
    1. Southern Baptist Convention--Doctrines. 2. Baptists--United
States--Doctrines. 3. Church--Unity. 4. Bible--Evidences, authority, etc. 5.
Bible--Inspiration. 6. Evangelicalism--United States. 7. Fundamentalism.
8. Church controversies--Southern Baptist Convention.   I. Title.

BX6462.7.S35   1993
286'.132—dc20   93-29725
                                                                             CIP

CONTENTS

Unless otherwise noted the scriptural quotations in this
volume are from the *New American Standard Bible*.

ILLUSTRATIONS

---

[1] The double-page Mainstream Affirmation is released from copyright so that it may be freely photocopied.

FOREWORD

For some of us the Southern Baptist Convention has been the central focus of our lives. We have been nurtured by what we think is one of the most remarkable denominations in Christian history. Our time, resources and very life have been devoted to it as the instrument of receiving and sharing the Christian Gospel.

It is true that some of us at times "kicked against the traces" and examined other Christian groups and perspectives. This is typical of spiritual as well as physical adolescents who are seeking to establish identity. We appreciate the fact that wise Southern Baptist leaders did not ostracize us but were patient and gave us room to study and examine other alternatives.

In most cases we returned with deeper appreciation of the genius and strength of our glorious Southern Baptist heritage of conservative theology, missions, evangelism, religious liberty, and social concern. We came to rejoice in the fact that we had various types of churches and worship styles within our distinctive parameters.

Because of our love for the Southern Baptist Convention the deep-seated conflicts of recent years have hurt many of us deeply. We have sought ways to restore unity and to learn from the rich diversity of our denomination. In the light of this context it is cause for rejoicing that Craig Skinner has written his splendid book which points the way toward the right type of unity.

Professor Skinner brings to his creative proposal a unique background. In his early years he was a leader among Australian Baptists. In addition to theological training in Australia he graduated from mainline U.S. Baptist seminaries of both the

North and South. He displays expertise in communication skills and holds his Ph.D. from an Australian State University in the area of Social Psychology of Education. Before joining our Golden Gate Baptist Theological Seminary faculty he taught in a leading "fundamentalist / conservative type" school. All of these experiences have given him a broad, informed perspective.

Dr. Skinner's book will help us with definitions. It gives us a social, psychological, and theological, analysis of different positions.

His work is based on solid biblical interpretation and theological wisdom. He has written in the spirit of the inerrancy conferences projected by the presidents of the six Southern Baptist seminaries.

The book opens new vistas of understanding. In addition to theological depth, this book is written with clarity in a non-polemic style. It is practical (note the ten commandments for unity). It should become the basis for prayerful study for individuals, leaders, and churches.

John P. Newport

Vice President for Academic Affairs
Emeritus Provost
Special Consultant for Academic Research to the President
Professor of Philosophy of Religion

Southwestern Baptist Theological Seminary
Fort Worth, Texas

HURTING AT THE HEART

In 1772 English Baptist Pastor John Fawcett wrote —

1. *Blest* is *the tie that binds*
   Our hearts in Christian Love;
   The fellowship of kindred minds
   Is like to that above.

2. *Before our Father's throne*
   We pour our ardent prayers;
   Our fears, our hopes, our aims are one,
   Our comforts and our prayers.

3. *We share our mutual woes*
   Our mutual burdens bear;
   And often for each other flows
   The sympathizing tear.

4. *When we asunder part*
   It gives us inward pain;
   But we shall still be joined in heart
   And hope to meet again.

5. *This glorious hope revives*
   Our courage on the way;
   While each in expectation lives
   And hopes to see the day.

6. *From sorrow, toil, and pain,*
   And sin we shall be free;
   And perfect love and friendship reign
   Through all eternity! *

But today's hymnals have changed the original first stanza to "Blest *be* the tie that binds...". What once began with a significant confession of evident blessing upon a present reality has now changed to a hopeful prayer for divine approbation.

Such mutations highlight the discords and divisions which form the deepest tragedy within our own denominational fellowships and among our transdenominational relationships.

As Fawcett's second and third stanzas so poignantly affirm we still share our common fears, hopes, aims, comforts, and prayers in many such contexts. We also echo easily the first few lines of his fourth stanza — for we do bear each others burdens with sympathetic sensitivity particularly in some local church associations.

But today we cannot follow that fourth stanza easily beyond the third line. For many of us, unfortunately, the hope to meet again seems deferred until eternity as our fellowship is broken because of divisions among us. We part too easily asunder. And we feel the inward pain because we still are joined in heart.

Schisms which separate us frustrate because our hearts hurt when we see true brothers and true sisters part. Across the doctrinal chasms yawning between us we discern others whom we feel share the common experience of salvation by grace through faith in Christ as Lord and Savior. We recognize that they may not agree completely with us in all matters but we still feel them to be part of our faith family and we hurt because fellowship is broken. Yet we hesitate to build bridges of restoration for fear that our integrity may be compromised.

I hold that the New Testament speaks clearly to such situations. Many gaps spread before us because some have adopted the unexamined assumption that uniformity of belief alone creates mutual unity. Like beliefs often do deepen fellowship. A measure of uniformity can often visualize oneness.

---

* This is the original 1772 published text (Julian: 1904:148). Later editors changed "is" to "be" in stanza # 1, and some also reworded stanza # 4.

But the idea that an absolute sameness of identical belief in all things is the only or even the major bond that ties us into spiritual association proves to be fictitious, non-biblical, and unworkable. In the pages which follow we shall examine this problem in the light of the New Testament and of social psychology. We do need a fresh evaluation of some biblical models. We also need to mark some of the parameters of our humanness clearly. We must all sharpen awareness of the limits which God has placed upon our spiritual association by our earthly state and its conditions.

Unless we are willing to work with faulty others as we are able (and as the Bible suggests we should) we stand in danger of aiming so high for the impossible that we can lose the possible. Striving for that which is the ideal can destroy our chance to possess the actual. Ultimate uniformity can only be ours when, with all other believers, we are finally conformed to the image of Christ in eternity. In that day our fellowship will have no limits. We are not exempted from the struggle to move towards such an entity during our earthly lives, but we need to be very careful that we are not striving for an ideal of total identity beyond earthly potentials.

No matter how we define the nature of functional unity we must recognize it to be something short of that ultimate and eternal ideal of conformity which some today appear to be feel should be achievable right now.

If we seek a responsible and practical unity today we must plan to include the stresses arising from our present imperfect and sinful human state. If the Lord intends for us to fellowship He surely expects this to be hammered out within the cultural and social matrix in which we exist. The needs for ministry, missions, evangelism, and other aching wants of our world must be balanced against the claims of individual rights to interpretation. We must factor in some room for a spiritual relationship for those Paul so well describes as — "All those who love our Lord Jesus Christ in sincerity" (Eph. 2:4) even though this may be slim and limited with some because their doctrinal differences loom so large.

Some of the practical questions we must face then are —

1. "What are the characteristics of the unity between believers which the Scriptures affirm we should seek?

3

2. What are the essential ties that bind us together in fellowship with others?
3. When and where do love and tolerance take precedence over separation?
4. What are the "bottom lines" in Christian agreements of fellowship?
5. Do these vary in differing situations?
6. What places do our attitudes, insights, focus, and behaviors hold in such relationships?
7. How can all these factors be brought to effective function within present situations?"

From many centuries of church history and from our own personal experiences we learn that co-operative fellowship within a local assembly of the Lord's people enables us to function as Christians much more effectively than ever we could in isolation. Local churches remain key units in God's plans for His people, and the chosen avenues through which He still reaches out to touch the world. Biblical models of co-operative fellowship beyond the local church suggest that the interdependence of churches need not limit their independence and autonomy.

Acts 15 records how early representatives from widely scattered congregations gathered to refine theological perspectives, and to discuss issues and problems of practical concern. Itinerant leaders from Jerusalem and Antioch taught, trained, and encouraged believers everywhere. They facilitated the appointment of locally elected leaders, and nourished the appropriate organization arising through such leadership.

Evangelism and missions in the New Testament appear as shared and co-operative endeavors. Brethren from a variety of localities gave prayerful (and often financial) support to those in other congregations having spiritual or material needs. The New Testament documents are all either resource materials about Jesus and the early church, gathered by individuals to be shared with others, or letters written directly to recipients in situations other than those of their authors. Thus a pattern of interdependency arises in the Scriptures as a strict corollary of independence. If local autonomy is the only operative principle without a larger co-operative fellowship then independence will always degenerate into isolation. In time of war today no individual family will draft its own soldiers, train, equip, send, supply, and support them on the battlefield.

In an organized world only an organized army can succeed. And organization is only the technical word we use for relationships. Wherever two or three gather in Christ's name a relationship exists. The major question is "What kind of a relationship should this be?" As we organize ourselves to relate to each so that we can complete the tasks of the kingdom best we find that the dynamic discovered in all spiritual association is that of simple supportive encouragement. We often do better together what we would have great difficulty doing well (or even at all) alone. We find the support and encouragement received from those who partner with us to be a major element in momentum as well as motivation.

Weaker churches need the support of stronger ones in denominational fellowship just as weaker Christians need the support of mature believers in the local church. Larger churches need the many channels for service provided by smaller churches if they are to actualize their potentials to help reach the world. Some local churches enlist leaders who need support beyond the local means in order to be able to serve the kingdom. Others have finances above their own needs to help in such endeavors. Denominational relations provide responsible channels whereby such disproportions can balanced to mutual benefit.

Of course a large individual church may help a smaller one through a one on one independent association. But unfortunately, more often than not, such a relationship can forge a directive component into the arrangement so that the weaker surrenders its autonomy to follow the dictates of the stronger (and often of its pastor or other power figures). The same difficulties may also arise when assistance comes through an association of churches or some other denominational board or agency.

But a denominational channel can reflect the whole mind of the churches much better than any individual resource. And where democratic organizational principles exist practical redress of any distortions can be better controlled and, where needed, more easily remedied.

If we hope to follow the principles encapsuled in biblical models and in the best of possible human relationships we need first to clarify the theological structures which will make them work. Such principles can then be adapted to function effectively locally, denominationally, and transdenominationally.

This does not mean we must adopt the concepts and simplistic slogans of popular ecumenics. But it does mean our minds must be open to the scriptural revelations on the nature of true spiritual unity. Most evangelicals, including Baptists, rightly oppose the ecumenical movement or are deeply disillusioned with it. Much ecumenical effort today lacks spiritual virility. Too often such programs display an anemic blandness from the wholesale blending of convictions around the lowest common denominators of belief. Because many of the ties that bind ecumenics appear to be so secular (and even "religious" rather than overtly Christian) many of their actions tend to be spiritually sterile.

In such situations we often find well-intentioned majorities, uncommitted to congregational and democratic ideals of co-operation, can ride roughshod over minorities. Too often valid emphases of the social and political dimensions to the Gospel displace its transcendent and spiritual realities. Some such associations seem to descend to simple levels of plain altruism. We must not allow such distortions of transdenominational fellowship to restrain our responsibilities in such areas. Where ecumenism has failed differing levels of local, denominational, and national co-operation may succeed.

The day of the denomination is not yet dead. Yet we are burned by the noontide heat and wearied with the burdens of the day. Our emotions strain as the age in which we minister stresses us often beyond the regular levels of human endurance. We tire and lose patience easily. We sometimes articulate our concerns clumsily and are often unaware of how our words hurt some of the family. We disregard the discipline that demands a constant fine tuning in all our relationships if fellowship is to survive in trying times.

We grab too easily for the quick and pragmatic answers and neglect to apply time-tested principles. For too long we have simply assumed that co-operative fellowship must build from a monolithic uniformity. We seek conformity, identity, and entity. I find none of these preconditions for co-operative fellowship taught within the Scriptures. Instead I discover unity, affinity, centrality, and compatibility. Spiritual association can only be authentic where such elements exist which can form adequate "ties that bind".

This study attempts to confront such concerns with courage. Of course no one work in this area can be final and potential abuses of every principle discussed abound. But the direction appears to be plain. Unless we face such dynamics, and are prepared to adjust our thinking as the Spirit may guide, progress may be impossible.

I obviously owe much to pastoral and academic associates, and to thoughtful lay persons and many others, for the ideas that have formed the foundation of my thought in these directions and refined them through their encouragement. Some reviewer's comments, and a foreword from a gracious senior theologian, arise from such sources. These must not be interpreted as affirming total agreement with every nuance of my argument of course. I cannot speak in behalf of all my fellow Southern Baptists, other evangelicals, or even my seminary colleagues.

Nevertheless I have found high interest and many affinities among all of these as the ideas developed herein have been shared previously in embryo. In the pages which follow the term "mainstream" is not meant to convey what is normally regarded as so "centrist" or "moderate" a position that it avoids all acceptance of any values from either side. (The analogy of one in the "mainstream" is well defined and explained by its use in the final section of this study, ["Prognosis"].)

I may clarify this idea further by changing the image to describe the position as that held by one who walks clearly among the majority. By so doing he or she travels right down the crown of the road, yet remains fully appreciative of real values to be gleaned from the paths chosen by others who walk beside — on both the right and the left.

From several quarters the movement towards a primary and mainstream emphasis which exalts Jesus Christ as Lord appears like some unexpected Gulliver, barely stirring from slumber, yet now miraculously cast upon the shores of our little kingdoms.

Should the full strength and momentum of this providence reach an early finality I believe it can be an effective agent of

7

true reconciliation. If Jesus Christ be truly recognized and obeyed as Lord that action has potential to be the catalyst which may well enable many more of our supposed enmities to be seen as the Lilliputian absurdities which some of them will always turn out to be.

Craig Skinner
Golden Gate Baptist Theological Seminary
Mill Valley, California, 94941.

1. Behold how good and how pleasant it is for brothers to dwell together in unity!
2. It is like the precious oil upon the head, coming down upon the beard, even Aaron's beard, coming down upon the edge of his robes.
3. It is like the dew of Hermon, coming down upon the mountains of Zion; for there the Lord commanded the blessing — life for ever.

— Psalm 133

1. I, therefore, the prisoner of the Lord, intreat you to walk in a manner worthy of the calling with which you have been called,
2. with all humility and gentleness, with patience, showing forbearance to one another in love,
3. being diligent to preserve the unity of the Spirit in the bond of peace.

— Ephesians 4

❦

DYNAMIC ONE: ATTITUDE

THE SPIRITUAL TIE —
UNITY NOT UNIFORMITY

*Experience is a good teacher, but she sends in
terrific bills.*

— *Mina Antrim*

For many years a famous television comedian, recently
deceased, introduced his weekly show with the dramatic
exclamation, "How sweet it is!" The cry always drew thunderous
acclamation. In the eyes of his audiences this man displayed his
talents as an entertainer so well, and obviously gained so much
pleasure from the performances himself, that they gladly affirmed
their identity with its "sweetness" through applause.

Life creates many such sweet associations between persons.
When a satisfying marital partnership emerges from young
people in love we find the intertwining of their interests and the
mutual meeting of their needs to be good for them, but also
pleasant for us to observe.

1. VALUING THE TIE THAT BINDS

The sweetness of mutual pleasure through a common
experience bonds us together with others. Where such an affinity
arises within in a meaningful situation the tie binds even stronger.
In the psalm quoted on the previous page David calls us to enjoy
the harmony of fellowship among God's family in similar terms.

Perhaps his inspiration arose from a recent experience of the spirit of love and harmony among the Lord's people when he felt the joy of unity at one of the great Jerusalem feasts? Then, when he returned, he took his harp and composed this, the shortest (but perhaps the sweetest) psalm in the whole biblical collection. Although only three verses long this short psalm forms a glorious hymn of praise to unity as the foundation of peace — and the tie that binds us best one to another.

The psalmist knew that simple association never guarantees harmony or good relationships. The book of Judges tells us how Sampson caught foxes, and tied them together in pairs by their tails with a burning firebrand between each pair. He certainly had some "fox-union" — but I am sure he had no "fox-unity"! The whole point was that the howling animals would pull this way and that, each loudly protesting at the indignity and discomfort of it all, and then zigzag through the enemies corn fields setting them afire and bringing them to ruin.

What is true about foxes appears more true about persons. Union cannot guarantee unity. We may tie ourselves with others through organization or other forced mechanical bonds but mere association cannot ensure fellowship. Unity arises from inward attitudes not from outward bonds.

UNIQUE EXPERIENCE

Nowhere else is unity among God's family better described nor illustrated than in Psalm 133. The first word "Behold!" (v. 1.) suggests the psalmist is alive with enthusiasm pointing a dramatic finger and crying "Hey! Will you look at this! Here is an experience rare and valuable."

He asserts the experience of unity among the family to be both unusual and almost unique in that it is both "good and pleasant". In life many matters hold moral value and many matters hold pleasure value. Unfortunately too many of the experiences which please us can be wrong — even sinful. And the good and worthy parts of life so often demand the kind of effort and discipline that brings discomfort and unhappiness. But an authentic family affinity possesses objective moral worth of itself as well as genuine enjoyment for those who share in it. We easily recognize how good it feels to discover real unity among brethren, and also how much pleasure and joy such an experience can engender. David presents two analogies illustrating the preciousness of such unity by recalling familiar pictures from history and nature.

EMBLEMS OF UNITY

The first emblem of unity selected is the anointing oil.(v. 2). Drawing his picture from Exodus 29:4-7 David reminds his people of the selection, separation and ordination of the national spiritual leader. This would be for most a rare and special experience perhaps witnessed only once in the average lifetime. Carefully chosen, expensively robed, and ceremoniously set apart the High Priest was then anointed with a preciously perfumed oil blended especially for the occasion. Searching for a way to underline the value of unity David urges us to cherish and prize it as we would a once in a lifetime opportunity to view a king's coronation, a president's installation, or the recognition of a spiritual leader selected by God from among all men in the nation.

Do we regard the experience of unity among God's people with such honor as that? Do we treasure authentic fellowship among God's family as the Jews would treasure their high priest? David sees such oneness as a fragrant and beautifying anointing which permeates the entire body.

The consecrating oil mingled myrrh, cinnamon, sweet calamus, cassia and other precious perfumes within an olive oil base. Thus they blended the bitter with the sweet, and the fragrant with the pungent into to a skilful union of diverse materials. God's people compounded this anointing oil just to pour it on the head of the high priest at his dedication in such abundance that it streamed down his face and beard. From the beard the fragrant flow continued through the upper opening of his robe collar saturating the whole garment even to its lowest hem. (v.2.). The mystery and glory of true spiritual oneness arises in part from its composite character. The fragrance of unity may saturate the whole although it be built from many blended elements.

The plus of unity among the family is a fragrant, refreshing and comprehensive experience. Here is an Old Testament picture of the New Testament experience of the anointing and refreshment of the Holy Spirit which comes to God's people in totality when they dwell together in unity.

Another emblem of unity selected is the refreshing dew of Mount Hermon. (v.3.). In the hot dry months between May and August in Palestine vegetation dries, flocks languish, and all life struggles. But regularly a soft Mediterranean mist in cool of early morning condenses on the tall mountains of Hermon and flows down the slopes to clothe the lower hills and valleys with green. This dewy refreshment feeds the tall cedars as well as the yellow corn. It brings life to the herds and flocks grazing in the mountains. It moistens the vines in the valleys and nourishes the lilies of the field.

The spirit of a unified brotherhood can be compared to the dew of Hermon. Some of the dew falling on the larger and taller mountains to the North of Jerusalem melted and diffused itself through the hills to run down to water and refresh the lands around Jerusalem bringing life and growth. Other moisture drawn up into the clouds from Hermon precipitated as refreshing showers to green the fields around Jerusalem in the mountains lower down.

Just as the flowing dew saturated the soil with the potential for life so the streams of unity flow among brethren reviving life, nurturing growth, feeding fellowship, bringing beauty and fruitfulness.

REQUIREMENTS FOR UNITY

From such analogies several affirmations naturally arise —

1. *No Unity Without Relationships*: By their nature soloists are individuals — they never promote harmony. The psalm celebrates the true joy of unity found as members of the same family "dwell together". (v.1.). True unity arises only as the family relates fully with each other and shares the fellowship of a common experience around a common Lord.

Unity binds us peacefully together through the harmonious ties of mutual interests and affections delighting us with its fraternity and its power. Unity means shared priorities in what we purpose, value and prize. Unity means shared feelings in that which we love, celebrate, and in what we delight. Unity means we share an authentic spirit of enthusiasm, faith, and commitment. Unity demands an intimacy in relationships and participative sharing.

2. *No Unity Without Liberty:* Members of the one family are

not clones. But they relate together in peace because, despite their individuality, each believes the factors that unite possess greater significance than the factors that divide. Unity demands harmonious variety. Fellowship in the family does not require a leveling uniformity where each loses all individuality and must think, feel, and act precisely as all others do. It cannot come from individuals each promoting only their own melodies. Unity is the blending of diversities not the encouragement of competing pluralities.

3. *No Unity Without Growth:* Peace reigns supreme in a graveyard. The dead do not strive or quarrel. A dead church can be peaceful enough but the live church, to be peaceful, must always be a place of life and therefore of growth. Times of refreshing from the presence of the Lord will come as the dews of heavenly blessing flow down. The Lord commands that blessing be where His people are (v.3.). and sends His Spirit down to flow even to the very edges of the fellowship where it is real.

4. *No Unity Without Fragrant Refreshment:* Authentic unity engenders celebration and worship, it permeates the fellowship with the perfume of joy. Artificial associations formally forced by creeds can only create a dry and outward form of oneness.

But the real unity of brothers and sisters is no mechanical result of mere association. Rather it arises from fellowship as an inner reality, warm, authentic and spiritual. Uniformity too easily becomes monotonous and wearisome but true unity always refreshes and beautifies. The pleasantness of unity among God's family is not only a delight to witness but is also a refreshing experience which nourishes the relationship and evidences its sweetness. Such a unity revitalizes us with spiritual nutrients which bring peace and foster spiritual life to its full strength.

While acts of uniformity may be the products of men genuine unity is the always the gift of God. Where each tree, bush, and hedge is clipped, cut, formed an fashioned into identical shapes there the beauty of the forest will be denied. Yet the variegated forest possesses unity for all its diversity as an affinitive grouping of green growing life fresh from the Creator's hand. It needs no formalized shaping to be such.

The oneness of the forest is a familial unity; one of similarity in origin; one of beauty of relation and proportion; one of value in individuality; and all with the purpose of glorifying God. Unity promotes worship, celebration, and joy. For the high priest the oil flowed from the head right to the outer skirts of his garment, for those in Zion the dew of lofty Hermon flowed down to meet all their needs with abundant blessing.

2. DIMENSIONS OF ENDEAVOR

The first three chapters of Paul's Ephesian epistle lay a groundwork of factual revelation concerning the church and its nature. Chapter four follows as the natural consequences arising from such foundations. The first word of chapter four "therefore" shows how the life of the church grows out of its core theology. By such a connection he insists that behavior grows out of belief. As a "prisoner of the Lord" Paul possessed the right to ask others for commitment and did so. Therefore, he exhorts his readers to live the kind of lives in relationship with other believers which honor such dedication. His challenge is to apply the truths revealed in ways which harmonize with our calling to be God's children.

We begin our thinking about unity best then exactly where Paul begins it. His call is to be "diligent to preserve the unity of the Spirit in the bond of peace". (v.3.). He gives us no invitation to create unity — this already exists if we are common members of the family of God. Our task is to foster unity, to maintain and encourage it.

Only the Holy Spirit can create the bonds of unity and peace. Our assignment is to realize how easily His work may be shattered by our thoughtless attitudes, and to commit ourselves to the responsibility of working hard to express and nourish the growth of greater unity within God's family. Paul sees the bond of peace which makes fellowship a pleasure as built on a unity which develops only through disciplined effort. (vv. 1,2). Right behaviors and right relationships within the family of God can only mature as its members restrain selfish human impulses and control themselves to express the four productive attitudes he names.

Humility: The first dimension Paul advocates is plain modesty or lowliness. This humility means simply to be more concerned about others before ourselves. It calls for each believer to be a modest unassertive self always looking for the blessing of others. Humility is not an expression of weakness but rather of strength. We see it best as modeled by Jesus who voluntarily surrendered His status as the Lord of all to identify with sinners by becoming one with us as a man, and to suffer as a substitute for our sins.

A member of God's family who seeks to preserve the unity of the Spirit in the bond of peace will not grasp for status or lord it over others. He or she will not seek personal glory but with true lowliness and humility will hold the first priority to be the welfare of the body and its other members.

Gentleness: Meekness or gentleness is the opposite of bad temper or roughness. The attitude is applied to Moses, and Jesus, and used throughout Scripture to identify the disciplined and mature individual gentle in spirit, able to bear pain and suffering, submitted to God in quiet restraint. The meek one is like a horse broken to the saddle with all of his strength and power present but tamed, controlled, useful, and serving needs outside of itself.

Patience: Patience is the spirit of caring in continuity; the ability to refuse to cease loving and helping others because of they fail or are weak. Impatient members of God's family sever relationships out of such frustrations and become harsh and judgmental of others. Elsewhere the apostle identifies it as a fruit of the Spirit (Gal. 5:22). This attitude of willingness to endure uncomfortable situations without irascibility is a courageous refusal to give in to anything that will destroy unity in the fellowship. It is a deliberate holding of oneself in control without passion. Divisions arise from our impatience as often as from anything else.

Longsuffering: Forbearance is that patience expressed in action. Paul defines it as motivated by love (v.2.) which ensures that we suffer others gladly and positively. Members of the family must not merely bear passively with the erring but should actively reach out all the while with positive efforts to restore broken unity and to strengthen the bond of peace.

Love suffers long and is kind (1.Cor. 13:4). So our longsuffering must not be given grudgingly, but willingly as part of our endeavor to walk worthy of our calling. Forbearance is not mere patience, it is patience which endures in continuity under frustrations and irritations.

While others hate, plot, or fail, ours is the privilege of pouring the alabaster box of perfume so that the fragrance of love can sweeten and permeate the mass. The short-tempered and quick to anger attack unity. The lowly, gentle, patient, and long-suffering build it. Constant sensitivity to others, full allowance for the frailties of human nature, and the preservation of a gentle even temperament combine to foster unity and peace.

Unity here is seen as part of the infrastructure of the Christian fellowship inherent in its nature. Unity is a "given". Unity is not an objective to be achieved but a possession to be guarded, a value to be maintained, a tie that binds to be strengthened. This unity of the Spirit in the bond of peace can only be preserved by our worthy walk. Peace should not be bought "at any price" but it can never exist unless we are prepared to meet its reasonable cost which Paul here declares includes a clear commitment to the practice of these four attitudes. We may discuss, even argue, over our differences but, if we truly are family we must disagree without being disagreeable.

3. THE BIBLE AND CRITICISM

The Bible remains largely silent concerning the authorship and date of many of its materials. Yet careful scholarly study can help us decide a great deal concerning them in addition to that which appears on the surface of the biblical content.

PROVERBS, JOB, DEUTERONOMY AND PSALMS

For example the book of Proverbs (in its present form) cannot have come directly from the hand of Solomon as is normally supposed by the uninformed. Chapter 25 informs us that Hezekiah and his company obviously added some of the present contents to the original. Other names are also mentioned as sources in the chapters which follow. Quite probably the ideas presented were originally Solomon's heard verbally by others, written down, and then brought together by some editorial hand into the present total collection.

Such information certainly does not negate Solomon as the

source of all the content, but it also indicates that we cannot simply say that Proverbs *in the form in which it now appears in our Bibles* comes directly from him. Other unknowns were involved in the transmission and probably in the editing.

The book of Job gives further illustration. It comes to us from an anonymous author. Job did not write it as in the final chapters he turns to trust in God's sovereignty without having any answers to his questions. He would possess some answers if he knew the information given us in the first chapter about his testing and Satan's accusations.

The first chapter seems to be in the form of a prologue, very similar to the introductory piece which might be spoken to an audience at a play who are told some facts of which the players in the drama are unaware. Like a dramatic piece the work continues through conversation and argument among participants. As in a play such dialogues reveal personalities as well as issues and problems to us. The characters appear as men representative of other men of every place and time.

We do not know the literary genius who took the story of Job and cast it into this dramatic form. This does not deny the validity of the story, nor lighten its value in any way. But it does show us the mark of an editorial hand somewhere.

Those who hold to the Mosaic authorship of Deuteronomy have good authority from the references of Jesus Himself. The Septuagint and other translations with which Jesus was familiar include the book as it now appears in our Old Testament and internal textual evidence supports the idea that Moses created its original form. (See 1:5, 31:26, 31:9). But only an ignorant person could claim that the story of Moses' death came from his own pen. Someone obviously added this after his decease, and most probably all of the final two chapters can be so understood.

So when Jesus quoted from the records and identified them as Moses' this was quite acceptable as it would be readily understood that for Moses to initiate the materials he would research and gather facts as any responsible author would. Within the first five books of our Bible we have many genealogical details (the 'begets'!) which probably came from other written records as their detail seems beyond the scope of merely oral tradition to memorize.

If Moses used such historical sources for genealogical

information he most probably also used other sources also for other historical materials. These could include orally-transmitted and written records. Those which cover Moses' own life are written in the third person not the first which, to say the least, appears unusual, if Moses is supposed to have penned them in the form in which they appear in our Bibles today. None of these assertions demand that we deny the essential Mosaic character of the original materials which we now know as Genesis through Deuteronomy. But they do illustrate how the most natural elements of responsible scholarship can cast valuable light upon biblical realities of authorship in a positive manner.

Similarly, the book of Psalms, as we now have it, can easily be seen as a reasonably late compilation, and not merely a much earlier grouping of those only written by David. During the exile, or shortly after it, some unknown hand gathered together 150 wonderful songs of praise and other expressions of spiritual exercise for the use of Jews who worshipped in the rebuilt Temple. In our current edition of this Hebrew hymn book the titles only identify 73 with David, and there is much debate as to whether the titles indicate that he wrote them, or that they were offered to his honor by others. Some others are identified either with Asaph, or the sons of Korah, or Solomon, or Moses. Many appear to be by unknown authors. Yet none of this necessarily detracts from the worth of individual psalms, nor of the collection. Neither is it wrong to speak of 'David's Book of Psalms' for 73:20 suggests that those identified with him at least were collated first, and they still stand as the core of the entire volume.

The above facts, simple as they are, suggest that positive values can arise from biblical criticism as much as negative ones. Such positive results of responsible scholarly analysis help us to understand how *some* of the Bible books (in the forms in which we now have them) are composite collations edited by unknown hands, and that the authors of some others cannot be determined. Such studies help support the naturalness of the revelation as given down the years by God through men and do not negate the Bible's truth or trustworthiness.

The heading above the book of Hebrews in many copies of the King James Version has traditionally ascribed its authorship to the apostle Paul, a view held by almost no contemporary scholar. It would be a very brave major publisher who could risk issuing a commentary on Hebrews claiming Pauline origins today and expect to retain integrity.

Even the "study Bibles" produced by "conservative" theological publishers include such results of literary and textual "criticism" along with others in their introductory notes to many of the Bible books. Comments like the following are as likely to be found now in *Moody Monthly* and *Decision* magazine as they are elsewhere.

> *The author of Judges-Ruth, which was originally one book, probably began with Joshua 24:28 (Joshua's death). Later Samuel added his history to the book, probably starting with David's family tree in Ruth 4:17 (1 Sam. 10:35). Nathan and Gad completed the history of David, starting with 1 Sam. 25:1 (Samuel's death; 1 Sam. 29:29-30).Samuel, Kings, and Chronicles, (originally one book each) cover 500 years of Hebrew history and were written as a continuous narrative by a succession of prophets (2 Chron.9:29, 12:15, 13:22, 20:34, 26:22, 32:32). (Hall,1987: 33).*

THE CRITICS AND CRITICISM

The use of the word "criticism" as a practice in biblical scholarship distresses some, particularly lay persons who have not had opportunity to study some technical areas of biblical understanding. But in biblical studies, as in other life experience, the word can be either positive or negative in attitude and outcome. "Criticism" exists as a neutral entity and means the process of evaluation of the level of quality or otherwise within a given piece of biblical literature. In times past scholars used "lower" criticism as the term to describe their evaluations of the most ancient biblical manuscripts from a textual perspective. "Higher" criticism sought to look beyond the text to understand the social, and cultural contexts, to identify the authors, and determine any editing through which the originals may have passed to reach the literary forms in which we have them today. The enormously helpful variety of translations which we possess today arise directly from such responsible studies. Their revisions and amplifications reflect many positive results.

POSITIVE OUTCOMES

The former differentiations of "higher" and "lower" evaluation have now coalesced into the one general description of the practice called "biblical criticism". This continues to express either a positive or negative character depending largely on the attitudes and pre-suppositions of the scholars who employ the discipline. (See Pinnock, 1984:Chap.6, for a clear discussion of how attitudinal pre-suppositions influence such results, also Reid, 1972).

Other effective evaluations (many of which include such contemporary areas of critical scholarship such as form criticism, source criticism etc.) also exist which when positively applied can be effective in the undergirding of orthodox perspectives. (Armerding, 1983; Bruce, 1959; Kitchen, 1966, 1977; Kline, 1963; Ladd, 1967). Unfortunately few on either side of the critical debate appear to be aware of some of these watershed studies.

Discoveries at Ebla, for example, well summarized by Kitchen (1977), yield firm linguistic data demolishing the carefully-constructed extremes of some German critics. These scholars dated certain Hebrew words as so "late" in history that they then were able to reject many Old Testament stories as later creations than they purported to be. The whole surmise of negative criticism in this area has been thereby shown to be built on a false foundation through the use of these disciplines by scholars with a positive (and conservative) orientation.

Even more significantly such corrections arose not from theologians, but mainly from the work of such secular orientalists and Egyptologists as Kitchen. His work which also details the impact of such data arising from archeological research in many other areas of biblical understanding appears, again, not to be noted much either by those on either extreme of the question of biblical veracity. (Cf. Pettinato, 1981.)

Some comments of a world-renowned Jewish Orthodox scholar about Old Testament truth summarize the situation well. Cyrus H. Gordon, Chairman of Mediterranean Studies and Professor of Near Eastern Studies at Brandeis University tells how he responded to some requests for such data and forwarded materials which detailed some of the fragile foundations of much of the hyper-critical hypotheses.

After he shared the facts Gordon was surprised to hear that his enquirer had decided to continue teaching in the older and more progressive system as he saw it stating —

> *... because what you have told me means I should have to unlearn as well as study afresh and rethink. It is easier to go on with the accepted system of higher criticism for which we have standard text books.* (Gordon, 1959)

Gordon's summary comment says it all —

> *What a happy professor! He refuses to forfeit his place in Eden by tasting the fruit of the tree of knowledge.* (Ibid.)

The answer to problems posed against faith through biblical criticism is neither to retreat into subjective defence nor to attack the whole idea of criticism as something in itself invalid. As Bruce says — "Where God's revelation is in view, no facts are inconvenient". (Bruce, 1959:10).

We must realize that many negative evaluations of biblical truth can arise from basic human and secular rather than spiritual assumptions. Those who begin their evaluations with naturalistic rather than supernaturalistic presuppositions ought not to be surprised if they end with negative outcomes.

Tenney sums it all well when he says —

> *Biblical higher criticism is not necessarily an assault on the Scriptures but is an examination of the historical and literary relation to the times and events concerning which they were written. The study is not in itself destructive: it can confirm and illuminate the biblical text just as well as it can cast doubt upon it or devaluate it. Insofar as historical and literary evidence can be used to find out exactly what the Bible means and to remove difficulties in understanding it, the study*

is beneficial. If it has been harmful the fault is
that of the critic rather than the method.(Tenney,
1960).

The question therefore resolves itself into a need to consider the presuppositions and assumptions with which both positive and negative critics foundation their rationales. We may begin such a consideration only by first examining the positive and negative beginnings in our approaches to the discovery of truth within the Scriptures. Inner attitudes can effect the outcome of our evaluations far more than is easily recognized.

4. THE BIBLE AND TRUTH

THE PROBLEM OF PRECISION

Baptists, along with many other evangelicals, traditionally agree on the necessity for religious liberty, and on the competency of all persons to relate as individuals directly to the Godhead through the merits of Jesus Christ (the doctrine usually described as "the priesthood of every believer"). We likewise hold to the autonomy and independence of each local congregation, and the right to interpret what God says to us through the Scriptures as individuals under the leading of his Holy Spirit.

The inspiration and authority of the Scriptures for all faith and practice stands as a central core for all of the above beliefs. It seems ethically impossible for a person to confess the above convictions without such a commitment to that focus.

But in these days many ask questions such as "How much actual precision exists within the biblical revelation? Are its statements objectively factual, exact, and accurate?"

In the minds of the majority who ask such questions they do not necessarily imply a serious reserve about biblical inspiration and authority but rather represent a serious attempt to define biblical inspiration and authority in order to facilitate our obedience to the biblical revelation.

Bible writers prepared their records factually and accurately as they perceived them under inspiration. But few today will wish to deny that some limits to their reports are imposed by the contexts and cultures of their times. Those who see certain passages which raise problems or other difficulties in these areas regard them mainly as reflections of the normal limits to be expected within human understandings.

To raise such questions does not necessarily infer rejection of the Bible as God's Word, unique, inspired, and authoritative. This simply expresses the very valid desire to understand and to interpret it in the most discerning and responsible manner possible.

Where today's readers struggle to reconcile what the Bible appears to say with contemporary understandings of history, science, or any other reality, such tensions as arise must be acknowledged as coming potentially because of two major concerns.

1. What we believe the Scriptures to be saying may differ from other contemporary understandings because our present knowledge remains incomplete.

2. What we believe the Scriptures to be saying may differ from other contemporary understandings because our interpretation of what we think the Bible means may be in error.

In the earlier days of literary criticism some scholars rejected all arguments which sought to support the Mosaic authorship of the Pentateuch simply because no writing was known to exist from that period. Subsequent archeological discoveries (including written records from well before Moses' time) have long since made rejection on these grounds now untenable.

On the other side of biblical precision the conservative traditionalists of the sixteenth century rejected Copernicus' theory about a heliocentric universe. They acted thus because they believed that the Bible taught that the sun orbited the earth. Our increasing knowledge reveals that such biblical expressions as were before understood as describing the sun rising and setting need now to be interpreted as poetic accounts of human experience rather than as precise and factual realities. (Although we all now know such descriptions to be scientifically incorrect we still talk of 'sunrise' and 'sunset' today because we talk of subjective experiential appearance and not in objective factual accuracy).

Thus our growing understandings of history and science have led to changes in positions once held both by progressives and conservatives in biblical interpretation. We have all learned that no matter how appearances are the present state of human understanding remains always incomplete and, accordingly, we can be mistaken in how we interpret exactly some of the factual data which the Scriptures seem to present.

The trustworthiness of a biblical record can often be supported through research and rational analysis. But any actual ultimate verification remains beyond the reach of such disciplines. How can we rationally validate materials from ancient times while our understandings of those original contexts and cultures always falls short of their full reality? How can we judge finally that what we think the Bible says is its actual statement when our interpretations may be distorted by truths as yet unknown to us?

If we use present day understandings to pass a final rational judgement upon the truth of anything we ignore the whole weight of human history which illustrates how we continue to advance in our grasp of truth with each generation. All our rational judgments must be tempered by this unstable nature of human knowledge. Fresh changes in tomorrow's understandings may effect the evaluations which seem so certain today.

Thus, if we limit our beliefs about biblical trustworthiness to only that which we can prove, difficulties we can reconcile, and problems we can explain, there seems no escape from a continually oscillating commitment. With every unexplained biblical difficulty our rational commitment to scriptural truth stands in jeopardy. When we face such tensions (and the most conservative of scholars admit them) we all commonly then revert to a faith statement. We indicate that we believe them to be reconcilable in the future through increasing knowledge, or to be understandable as our increasing interpretations of them improve.

INSPIRATION AS A FAITH ASSERTION

This leads me to the belief that trust in the inspiration and authority of the Scriptures must always be, at heart, *a faith assertion*. My plea is that we accept that kind of faith assertion as the basis for all commitment to biblical inspiration and authority rather than just to flee to it only when contemporary rational thought offers no final resolution.

Unless the attitude of the Bible student is one which begins with the assertion by faith that it is God's Word, inspired and authoritative, he or she will constantly oscillate between holding this position by reason, and rejecting it by reason. As noted above in the past some negative critics rejected any idea of Moses' writing anything because at that point they knew of no writing to be extant which could scientifically be dated as from his time. On the other hand some more positive traditionalists rejected a scientific view of the universe because they misinterpreted some biblical poetic statements as factual ones. Subsequent knowledge has forced changes in both views. Human reason will always force such oscillations because human knowledge continues to change so much. Only a view of inspiration and authority which is based on simple faith can be a stable one.

From such a basis we can rejoice in corroborative materials from present day knowledge, and also be unembarrassed by seemingly irreconcilable difficulties. We are not excused from the responsibility of careful scholarship and harmonization, but our pledge to biblical veracity remains independent of such efforts. Faith, as always, is not irrational. But it cannot depend solely on arguable logic else it will cease to be faith and become only reason. And human reason will always be limited, incomplete, and unsatisfying.

God's family need not be discomforted by the call to such a faith perspective. If it seems paradoxical to hold to the inspiration and authority of the written word without a totally logical rationale this is no different than the call to hold that Jesus Christ is both human and divine.

For many centuries the church struggled to reconcile these two seemingly opposing perspectives of Jesus' character but finally accepted the fact that the doctrine of Christ's Person is to be believed rather than reasoned. Human intellects operate under a system of logic that will not allow the same person to be both God and man, yet we accept this truth as a revealed reality about Jesus. In a similar manner our minds can take in salvation from God's perspective as an eternal election and choice of the individual.

Alternately, we may view salvation from man's perspective as a free-will responsibility of the individual through faith.

But we do not reject either of the above doctrines because we cannot rationally reconcile them.

We accept them as paradoxes in terms of the limits to our human rational thought, and we find that we can best function as God's family in this world by so believing.

SOME ASSUMPTIONS OF LOGIC

An understanding of the place of axioms in human thought may assist us to exercise such faith in the Bible's inspiration and authority. Each person "sees" various matters in very particular ways. Heredity, environment, our own choices and experiences, and many other individual factors help shape the specific personality. Most of us reason logically, but few among us readily recognize the foundations upon which our rational thoughts develop.

We all adopt unexamined bases for rational thinking and often remain unaware that such assumptions continue to condition the paths along which our logical thoughts will move.

The philosophers call such beginnings, and leaps of faith, *axioms*.

The axiomatic method, first enunciated by Aristotle, and followed by Euclid and virtually every other philosopher, affirms that no system of logical reasoning about any matter can exist unless it argues deductively from a basic given or "axiom" (from the Greek *axioun* (:"to think worthy"). In each case, however, (whether these are common notions intuitively held by all humankind or purely assumed postulates or principles) the character of an axiom is such that it exists as the primitive proposition with which one must begin in developing an particular "line" of reasoning.

Such assumptions always lie beyond the range of normal, logical, human proof. (Reese, 1980:45-46, *New Encyclopedia Britannica,* Vol.1, 1986:747). Axioms are assumptions postulated as a foundation for logical thought.

An axiom is a truth, self-evident to the proposer but not necessarily to those to whom his proposition is made, and therefore (in the proposer's mind) not ever debatable. It is assumed, without proof, for the sake of the consequences which flow logically from it through rational discussion.

At first sight we may deny that such assumptions exist for

our logical reasoning but we can easily note their force in everyday mathematics (the purest form of reasoning) by considering the geometrical reality that "a straight line is always the shortest distance between two points", and the arithmetical reality that "two plus two equals four". Both of these seemingly basic truths turn out to be unprovable postulates in that other "givens" lie behind each of them. We can illustrate the practical applications of some such beginning assumptions but they cannot be proven as they stand by pure reason alone. Each such axiom is a presupposition which carries within its character a belief assertion. Each is therefore subject to challenge.

Normally a straight line does provide the shortest route between two points but for this to be rationally true we must *assume* that both points sit on a level surface and in the same plane.

But if the two points are cities around the globe they sit on a spherical surface. Then the shortest distance between them may well be the curved line which follows the circularity of the earth as every air passenger who has flown from New York to Europe over the Northern ice route knows.

Behind this (apparently) undebatable statement then lies the unproven and hidden assumption that we are discussing plane rather than spherical geometry, as the latter possesses no straight lines at all!

The logic which applies to curved surfaces works from different axioms. It requires a different set of given assumptions to be rational.

Again, two apples plus two ideas will never total four of any thing specifically. We actually, then, began our "logical thinking" about "twos" with the unrecognized and unproven assumption that we were considering like entities such as numbers, fruit, concepts, etc.

From another aspect even two "numbers" may not always equal four. We assumed (without any discussion) that the numbers in question were "units".

But if one set of the "twos" are double units (2s), and another set of the "twos" are "two hundreds" (200s), then two of the first plus two of the second will equal an arithmetic four hundred and four units not just "four".

When asked how he discovered his famous theory of relativity professor Albert Einstein simply answered "I challenged an axiom!" All axioms are open to such challenge. They exist as presuppositions essential for logical argument to flow. They undergird all rational thought and often enter into it largely unrecognized. But they are all inner attitudes about truth which we choose to adopt without proof.

As the bases of our own individual thought appear so self-evident to us we often fail to recognize how others can erect a logical argument using different assumptive bases which are equally self-evident to them. While their conclusions may differ from ours the actual nature of any opponent's reasoning is normally exactly the same as ours as it begins with unprovable givens (and often adds others *en route*) just as our reasonings do.

The atheist may begin with the philosophical axiom (self-evident for him or her) which asserts that there can be no personal God and therefore no revelation of Him is possible. Given that kind of assumption as a faith-foundation for thought then the rest of atheistic reasoning about the universe is not necessarily "illogical" — even if the conclusions are wrong!

THE CHRISTIAN AXIOM

Christians begin with the axiom (self-evident for them) that a perfect and personal God reveals Himself to men in Jesus Christ. The Bible proclaims that such a faith-assertion is the key to all knowledge and constructive thought about God (Heb. 11:6).

Both the atheist and the Christian axioms are matters of personal choice and clearly illustrate that the difference between those who know God, and those who do not know Him, rests squarely on such volitional and assertive foundations.

Scholars divide over whether the coming of Christ into human flesh involved a certain reduction of His deity or not. Some interpret the biblical material as indicating that the revelation of God in Christ was not a perfect one in the sense of telling us all there is to know about God. But they believe His revelation to be as complete as we could receive it. They say that it appears that, while the divine nature and attributes remained in Christ's human person, the incarnation brought with it some voluntary self-limitations.

Thus Jesus could be human when he was weary, thirsty and

hungry, yet also express astonishment at the faith of the centurion and at the unbelief of the men of Nazareth. Mark 13:22 certainly suggests some limits to His knowledge while in the flesh and Phil. 2:5-11 talks of His self-emptying.

Yet He also knew the inner thoughts of some men and women and commented on their personal histories from larger than human perspectives. Others therefore claim that all the biblical materials which talk of Christ's emptying Himself and becoming poor relate only to His laying aside of divine dignity and glory, and not to any casting aside of divine attributes and powers.

They say we cannot claim that the man Christ Jesus could be fully God if He lacked any of the qualities of deity, and that to reveal the Father demands a perfection of nature in His Person with no limitations. (For an helpful discussion of these concerns see Packer, 1973:51-56.)

Whatever perspective of the Kenotic theory (the theological name for the problem of Christ's human nature as outlined above) one determines to believe one fact remains unchanged. While Christ came as truly God and truly man we cannot escape from the reality that the revelation we have is one of God veiled in human flesh. However we may regard the incarnation we must always view our understandings of God which arise from it as still partial, incomplete, and yet to be expanded.

As He departed Christ told us that much more about His declaration of the Father would continue to become clear to us as the ages progress through the work of the Holy Spirit. When He left us He emphasized how much more we still needed to know when He said "I have many more things to say to you but you cannot bear them now". He then promised that the work of the abiding Holy Spirit would be to expand, clarify, and increase our understandings of all that had been already given in the Son (John 16:12-14).

The Holy Spirit's enlargement of the meaning of Christ's revelation continued through Acts and through the ministry of the apostles, and still continues today. So the best we may say about His coming is that while we may never understand perfectly all the truth about God in Christ nevertheless we shall possess that perfect revelation in fullness one day.

Although we may not perceive all the truth right now then, nevertheless all that we do know is truth. So the understanding of God known through Christ by us at any time is truth as we are able to receive it, and this is perfectly suited to our needs now yet not yet the total revelation of God. That revelation in its fullness awaits the time when we shall move from knowledge in part to "knowing as we are known", and to the maturity of spiritual stature which will be ours when we see Him "as He is" and are fully like Him. (1 Cor. 13:9-12, 1 John 3:1-3).

When we talk of the revelation in Christ as final and complete for men now we discuss its power to function rather than its objective absoluteness understood fully by us without limitation. Imperfect as our understandings of God in Christ may be they nevertheless remain adequate for our needs.

DIVERGENT REASONING

"Progressives" and "conservatives" in theology both begin with the axiom of a genuine value of the revelation in Christ to meet our human needs. They both then alike diverge from this base as they adopt other unproven axiomatic assumptions into their reasoning, often rather unconsciously.

Such positions are so linked with our individual ways of "seeing" things that they may often confuse us into thinking that one way of reasoning appears more logical than another. But if one position is to be valued more than another the assumptions within that position must be shown to be more rationally worthy than the other. And this seems almost impossible as our axioms reflect our personal choices rather than our reasoned conclusions.

I may consider another's faith assertions as less correct than mine, or less worthy than mine, but I cannot help him or her see this by logic and argument alone. Axiomatic foundations always remain as choices of the human will.

The table which follows below compares the two major flows of logic arising from the foundation of biblical revelation, and shows how "leaps of faith" occur throughout each of them.

Given the assumptive bases with which each begins, and the other axiomatic suppositions introduced throughout, both lines of reasoning reach the conclusion that faith in the inspiration and authority of the Scriptures is valid!

Neither can negate the other's position as "unreasonable" as each uses axiomatic leaps to begin and continue their discussions. While these appear self-evident to their users they actually exist without proof as assumptive postulates which (for each of them) are not open for debate as far as the logical development of their rationales is concerned.

The common axiom of faith with which all Christians begin is —

In Jesus Christ, His Son, a perfect, personal God displays Himself finally in a human revelation which, although we may only understand it partially, is nevertheless sufficient to meet the needs of our human condition.

TABLE OF AXIOMATIC RATIONALES

"Progressive" Logic

1. This revelation, because it comes through human men and women will include some personal misunderstandings and inaccuracies in areas of history and science.

2. Because of limits to our present understandings interpretations of what the revelation actually says may also be inaccurate.

3. Nevertheless the Scriptures, as we now have them, are totally trustworthy in all matters of faith and practice.

4. From our perspective the above constitutes an high view of biblical inspiration and authority as it expresses a faith in these despite the difficulties observed.

"Conservative" Logic

1. Although this revelation comes through human channels it does not necessarily follow that personal misunderstandings and inaccuracies have to be reflected therein in factual matters.

2. Although limits exist these need not restrict our interpretation of any realities.

3. We can only hold legitimately to trustworthiness in faith and practice as we also exercise a similar faith in the factual understandings of biblical revelations of history and science.

4. From our perspective the above constitutes an high view of biblical inspiration and authority as it expresses an acceptable rationale for a faith in that doctrine.

In both of the preceeding columns "leaps of faith" are evident in virtually every step of the "logic"! Those who reason with the left column suppose that our human condition imposes limits which affect factual matters as they are communicated to us or reflected upon by us. Those who reason with the right column suppose that such human limits impose no such restrictions upon such realities. Each rationale appears to be equally defensible from its appropriate axiomatic beginning.

But either of the assumptive bases named as Nos. 1, 2, or 3 above, also reflect the wilful choices of the proponents and are equally logical *for them* from the axiomatic acceptances from which they choose to see such matters. As each rationale proceeds proponents appear to add these axiomatic elements which they assume others will share — but which they do not seek to prove and cannot.

When a lay person hears of these kinds of tensions among theologians and denominational leaders on the nature of the Bible he or she is tempted to feel that it must be that some deny inspiration and some affirm it. The struggle is not so much between a positive and a negative view of biblical inspiration however, but rather one over how the doctrine of biblical inspiration can best be conceptualized and defined.

It sometimes appears as if the fight is over biblical inerrancy among Southern Baptists, but we seem rather to have a difference about just how inerrancy can be defined. Is it to be stated in an elaborately 'tight' manner such as in the right column of the "conservatives" above or presented in a more open and permissive way such as appears in the left column favored by "progressives"? (Cf. *Proceedings...* 1987:77). James I. Packer and many of the other leading inerrancy advocating evangelical theologians pay adequate attention to such scholarly concerns about its nature. They very clearly state some major limitations and exclusions which must be accepted in any claim that the Bible in the present verbal form in which it exists is perfectly clear in its communication of factual accuracy. The well-known *Chicago Statement on Inerrancy* which they have authored allows for much that is cultural, editorial, poetic and unclear in the present text yet still affirms that we may trust its truthfulness. (Cf. Appendix A,).

Fisher Humphries has thoroughly illustrated how this

statement modifies the "tight" view of inerrancy with many careful qualifications. He demonstrates that it adds little to the *Baptist Faith and Message Statement* already common to Southern Baptists, and that it also allows for a variety of interpretations of the word "inerrancy". (Humphries, 1986).

As Pinnock has further said, (when (addressing those of differing positions within S.B.C.) —

> *The irony of it is that the Chicago statement, which the militants say they endorse, encompasses both your positions. Like the militants it speaks of complete errorlessness but like the moderates it also speaks of the lack of technical precision and the topical arrangement of material and such like. (Proceedings..., 1987: 77)*

Many wish to substitute all kinds of other statements for the terms inerrancy and infallibility. Yet these words remain as the most useful bit of theological shorthand we can use if we do so responsibly. There seems therefore good warrant for retaining them where possible as, in today's climate, the substitution of other terms tends to suggest that the writer or speaker is somehow attacking biblical integrity.

A major dictionary (such as the *Oxford Dictionary of the English Language,* etc.) will show that while "inerrant" means simply without fault or error, "infallible" carries some additional implications. It means not expected to prove false in the sense that it is not liable to fail in its function, action, or operation. While inerrancy refers to truthfulness in *content* infallibility refers to truthfulness in *action*. (Helpful mainstream contemporary discussions of the whole inerrancy question can be found in Erickson, 1983: 22-240; Henry, 1979: Vol.1V, 201-219; and Honeycutt, 1986.)

A MAINSTREAM APPROACH TO INSPIRATION

With such understandings in mind one helpful way out of such an *impasse* may be to define the inspiration of the Scriptures as meaning that they are *contextually inerrant and functionally infallible* .

For any doctrine of inspiration and authority to be practical it will need to include room for both the above ideas and to express them in such terms as are open for adoption by "progressives" as well as by "conservatives". 'Contextually inerrant and functionally infallible' is a mainstream approach to the need for a positive statement about biblical inspiration whose meanings can be defined as follows.

1. Contextually Inerrant : This description affirms that the Bible as we have it, when interpreted in the light of its original cultures and contexts, is a completely trustworthy and authoritative revelation of God containing truth without any mixture of error.

2. Functionally Infallible : This description affirms that the Bible, as we have it, when responsibly proclaimed, is an effective instrument in the hands of the Holy Spirit enabling its hearers to fulfill the Father's will.

Accordingly, as well as claiming the Scriptures to be entirely trustworthy in their facts we also view them as effective in function, and adequate in form to fulfill the purposes for which they have been given.

These are perspectives which allow us to accept the value and trustworthiness of the biblical revelation and to apply their teachings just as they are. Unlike the *Chicago Statement On Inerrancy* the above two descriptions form a simple interpretive definition which centers on the actual Bible which we possess and not upon some original autographs to which no one has access.

To affirm that the Bible as we have it is contextually inerrant and functionally infallible require us to view the materials positively and responsibly yet also demands that we include a balanced understanding of the place of our human limitations.

A most important matter to note here is that such a claim does not infer that there is no erroneous factual information as judged by contemporary knowledge recorded in the Bible. As article XIII of the Chicago Statement states —

> *We further deny that inerrancy is negated by biblical phenomena such as lack of modern technical precision, irregularities of grammar*

or spelling, observational descriptions of nature,
the reporting of falsehoods, the use of hyperbole
and round numbers, the topical arrangement of
material, variant sections of material in parallel
accounts, or the use of free citations. (Chicago
Statement ... Appendix, Article XIII).

Several authors have demonstrated how easily such factual difficulties" in the biblical record can be reconciled. (Archer, 1979; Boice, 1984: chap.5). Even where the error persists it may lose any significance and relevance it appears to possess and matter no more when explanations yet to come clarify the sense of the records in terms of their contextual understandings.

Thus critics who see error in Jesus' statement about the mustard seed being the smallest of seeds point out that we now know of other seeds today which are smaller. So Jesus' statement is not absolutely true for all ages and for all time. In the absolute sense it is, and will remain an "error". But He shared this as understandable truth in relation to the experience of His hearers. So our grasp of the contextual time and culture of its delivery makes the factual imprecision totally insignificant even though the "error" still persists in an absolute sense.

Quite a number of the so-called "difficulties" can either be resolved or reduced to such insignificance rather easily and one is continually amazed at their triviality and encouraged to believe that others will finally appear likewise.

Stating a belief in contextual inerrancy declares the conviction that only when we know the perspectives of biblical writers fully, and understand the totality of all the textual realities and their transmissions, shall we truly understand all the details of the record.

We cannot claim that the present historical and scientific facts recorded in the Scriptures exist in such a form that we can be certain to grasp them fully now in terms of our contemporary understandings. As we find more about the cultures and contexts of their production we find ourselves forced to change some initial interpretations about what we first thought was being said. The great bulk of these changes have simply clarified the revelation for us.

So we increasingly learn that our knowledge was partial, our analyses faulty, and our understandings incomplete. This is mostly so because of the historical intellectual, and philosophical distances between ancient peoples and ourselves.

Regarding the Scriptures then, as contextually inerrant, sees them as trustworthy yet not exempt from misunderstanding by us. Such a view regards them as accurate factual records within the locus of their production but allows for the resolution of any apparent difficulties when all is known at the end of time.

By such a statement we confess our belief that when we understand fully how to interpret the Scriptures all of their truth will be evident. We may clarify many such difficulties through careful study while in this life but a final certitude about any or all of them will await eternity.

From that knowledge we shall then be able ultimately to interpret the entire revelation correctly and any so called factual "errors", while they may remain, will be shown to be not inharmonious with the revelation. Final evaluations should be postponed until then. We have seen enough supportive evidence of the Bible's accuracy thus far through our increasing understandings that to make such a faith-assertion that we shall understand it all one day is a reasonable and logical affirmation.

As the Bible calls for faith in God and in His revelation the validity of accepting its inspiration and authority by faith exceeds that of merely treating it as a collection of literature to be examined for errors and fallacies. The way of approach to any truth must always be conditioned by its nature and, according to Hebrews 11:4, faith is the only valid way to understand God or His word.

> *A flower may be approached by a bee to find nectar in it, or by a butterfly to rest on it, or by a botanist to determine its classification, or by an artist to paint it, or by a chemist to analyze it. Certainly the Bible can be studied as literature and as history as well as divine communication. But we must take into account how the Bible wishes us to approach it and for what purpose. It obviously wants us to come to know God in Jesus Christ. Therefore we are within our epistemic rights as Christians when we insist on approaching the Bible in the spirit of faith. (Proceedings...,* 1984: 133).

So the term "functionally infallible" will also be a faith-assertion. This expresses our belief that realities reflected in the text are sufficient to fulfill the purposes for their existence as we have them whether fully understood or not.

As far as I can determine only one verse of Scripture even suggests anything about the *process* of inspiration, "Men, moved by the Holy Spirit, spoke from God" (1 Pet. 1: 21). The context of vv.16-21 (and also the insights from 1 Pet. 2:10-12), throw some light upon this statement. All other biblical comments restrict themselves to a discussion of the facility of theScriptures to function effectively.

Christ clearly enunciated the major purpose which the Scriptures serve when He told the Pharisees that they erred believing that spiritual life came from these words. Jesus said their function is to point to Him and to testify of Him. (John 5:39)

The biblical materials then must primarily be seen as instruments which function to reveal Jesus Christ and to effect God's Will. The focus of the Bible's teaching about itself is a declaration that its authority and inspiration form a result which functions unfailingly. The Scriptures seem to be quite silent about the process whereby they came to be what they are.

Why should we argue so much about the process by which the result exists when our main task is to employ God's word for the purposes for which it is given? These purposes include the power of the Scriptures to make us wise unto salvation (2 Tim. 3:15). They also embrace the effectiveness of their function as tools to do God's work. As I use the Scriptures I find that they do cut with a power sharper than a two-edged sword and they are able to judge the thoughts and intents of the human heart (Heb. 4:12).

The Bible is given to teach, reprove, correct, and train us (2 Tim. 3:16), and to plant faith and increase assurance (John 20:30-31, Rom. 10:17, 1 John 5:13). We are not compelled to understand all about the origin of the Scriptures or to define their character with absolute exactness in order to receive them and apply them with faith. As Thomas Edison is reputed to have said —

> *We don't know the millionth part of one percent*
> *about anything. We don't know what water is. We*
> *don't know what light is. We don't know what*

gravitation is. We don't know what enables us to keep on our feet when we stand up. We don't know what electricity is. We don't know what heat is. We don't know anything about magnetism. We have a lot of hypotheses about these things, but that is all. But we do not let our ignorance about all these things deprive us of their use.

Where it is not possible to understand all about the Bible's origin and development, or to define every aspect of its nature, we may still exhibit faith that the proclamation of God's Word as it is, and the explanation of it as best we can, fosters faith. "Faith comes by hearing, and hearing by the word of God" (Rom. 10: 17.)

Faith is not born from rational analysis, nor created by verifiable argument and discussion. All of these may buttress faith, but faith itself arises as a heart response to the proclamation the revelation of God's Grace through Jesus Christ declared in His written Word.

Thus the primary validation of the Bible's veracity lies in its demonstrated ability so to function effectively and not by any philosophical theory or through any rational analysis of its nature. The authenticity of the Scriptures, then, appears as a faith-reliance reality and as a personal response to the Bible's own claims for itself. The proven effectiveness of the Bible's ability to fulfill the purposes of its intention validates it to be God's own Word. (Isaiah 55:10-11)

Billy Graham's official biographer tells of the young evangelist's dilemma just before his ministry came to prominence through the Los Angeles Crusade in 1949. A close companion (Chuck Templeton) who was in the process of abandoning his faith, talked much with him about the many problems raised by liberal scholars about biblical truth.

Mr. Graham struggled with many of those unresolved difficulties and wondered just how he could continue to proclaim the Scriptures with the confidence that they could be spiritually effective. (Pollock, 1966:77-81) In desperation one night Billy read again the biblical passages which affirmed its inspiration and authority. Finally, deep in prayer, he wandered out into the forest adjoining the spiritual conference center where he was a featured speaker that week.

He saw that intellect alone could not resolve the question of authority. He must go beyond intellect. He thought of the faith used constantly in daily life: he did not know how a train or a plane or a car worked but he rode them. He did not know why a brown cow could eat green grass and yield white milk, but he drank milk. Was it only in things of the Spirit that such faith was wrong? He later said,

> So I went back and got my Bible, and I went out into the moonlight. And I got to a stump and put the Bible on the stump, and I knelt down, and I said, "Oh. God; I cannot prove certain things. I cannot answer some of the questions Chuck is raising and some of the other people are raising, but I accept this Book by faith as the Word of God". (Pollock, 196: 81)

He stayed by that stump praying wordlessly, his eyes moist.

> I had a tremendous sense of God's presence. I had great peace that the decision I had made was right'. (Ibid)

The Los Angeles Crusade which followed immediately developed as the turning point in his whole ministry. "He stopped trying to prove that the Bible was true and just proclaimed its message". (Pollock, 1966:93)

Later, in London, Graham made his own statement about the value of the Bible's functional infallibility.

> "There is authority", Graham told the clergy, "when this Book is quoted, and the more Scripture that I quote the greater number of people come and respond to the invitation. I found that out night after night. The Word of God, even though the hearer doesn't understand all about it, somehow becomes a hammer and a sword that hurts and cuts and convicts and washes and cleanses — the quoted Word of God". (Pollock, 1966:169).

The ideas capsuled in the recommended phrase "contextually inerrant and functionally infallible" are well summarized by Baptist author Erickson in his fine new evangelical theology.

> *The Bible, when correctly interpreted in light of the level to which culture and the means of communication had developed at the time it was written, and in view of the purposes for which it was given, is fully truthful in all that it affirms. (Erickson, 1983: 233-234).*

5. UNITY NOT UNIFORMITY

Thus far we have seen how unity among God's people builds from the positive attitude which works from the given reality of unity rather than one which aims for uniformity. A view of the kingdom which demands that each be exactly alike so that the whole stands as an as a uniform whole without variety cannot be sustained from the Scriptures.

In his great discussion of the coming of Christ in Philippians 2 Paul echoes his Ephesian counsel about humility, gentleness, patience, and longsuffering. Among the elements of the unity of the Spirit and the bond of peace which tie us together in God's family he speaks of the need for its members to "Do nothing from selfishness or vain deceit, but with humility of mind let each of you regard one another as more important than himself" (Phil. 2:3).

Paul considers that believers who are thus first concerned for the interests of others above themselves (v.4) reflect the attitude modeled by Christ (v.5). And in this passage he also calls for a unity of mind, love, spirit, and purpose (v.2). He bases his pleas for such unity on the foundational affinities we possess as a common family naming these as our oneness in Christ, our mutual affection, our sense of partnership, and our compassion for the weak among us (v.1).

From these, and many other like passages (Rom. 12:6, 15:4-5; 1 Cor. 1:10; 2 Cor. 13:11; Col. 1:10-11, 3:12- 13; 2 Tim. 2: 24-25; James 1:4,19) we find attitude to be all important in the preservation of unity. The inner mind-set, the spiritual orientation of the individual, governs that person's behavior and therefore enables him or her to walk worthily or otherwise. Only a basic attitude of co-operation which prizes the unity between all of God's children will allow us to walk worthy of our calling to preserve the bond of peace.

The tie that binds us together cannot be found through a totality of identical agreement on everything. It must begin where the Bible begins with the cultivation of an attitude that places others and the interests of God's family above our own. The good and pleasant peace of fraternal unity builds from a harmony created as we see the preservation of the place of others as primary. Where the attitude of the individual Christian is a mind-set which seeks to preserve fellowship the family relationships will be characterized by humility, gentleness, patience and authentic longsuffering. We are called to be "diligent to preserve the unity of the Spirit in the bond of peace" and told that this can only come through the disciplined application of these Christian graces. These ties will bind, not through each member of the body reaching an identity with every other, but rather by the upbuilding of a unity which transcends the differences to encourage harmony. Where our commitment is to the preservation of that unity among the fellowship of God's people even the difficulties raised by some negative biblical criticism can be balanced by the many values supported by the positive uses of that discipline.

Various views of the process by which the Scriptures came to us ought not to be divisive concerning their ultimate authority and inspiration. This is because, while each of the conservative and progressive views of such processes develops its own logic, each adopts unprovable axioms similar to each other in their assumptive character. Yet each perspective can lead equally to the conclusion that the Bible is trustworthy, a result which must always be seen as a faith assertion and not merely as a fully reasoned one.

One poet pictures the effect attitude can have on outward results through a striking verse written between New Haven and New York on the steamer *Richard Peck*. She composed it upon hearing her husband's comment that the sailboats around them angled their sails so that they either travelled east before the sea winds, or sailed west by tacking against them.

One ship drives east and another drives west,
  With the self-same winds that blow.
'Tis the set of the sails and not the gales
  Which tells us the way to go.
Like the winds of the sea are the waves of fate,
  As we voyage along through life:
'Tis the set of a soul that decides its goal,
  And not the calm or the strife.
  — *Ella Wheeler Wilcox (1855-1919)*
  Morrison, 1948: 314

An attitude which demands uniformity in all things can sunder fellowship. But the individual who seeks unity will not allow differences to separate. Through humility, gentleness, patience and longsuffering we may all nourish the peace which becomes a tie that binds and allows us to move along well driven by the wind of the Spirit. And the attitude which endeavors to preserve unity can be a dynamic which forms a spiritual tie between believers. In the next chapter we shall examine another bond — the family tie of common experience — which also nourishes our endeavor to preserve that unity.

14. As a result, we are no longer to be children, tossed here and there by waves, and carried about by every wind of doctrine, by the trickery of men, by craftiness in deceitful scheming:
15. but speaking the truth in love, we are to grow up in all aspects into Him, who is the head, even Christ,
16. from whom the whole body, being fitted and held together by that which every joint supplies, according to the proper working of each individual part, causes the growth of the body for the building up of itself in love.

— Ephesians 4

❦

Dynamic Two: Insight

The Family Tie — Affinity Not Entity

A moment's insight is often worth a life's experience.
— Oliver Wendell Holmes

Previously (Eph.1:22-23) the apostle has described the church as the body of Christ, now (4:4a) he enlarges that figure and speaks of the church's unity as "one" linked through the "one" Holy Spirit. Christ is likened to the head and each individual to a member of that one body.

1. The Christian Family

The image of the church as a body stresses the common life we share in Christ. Believers are said to have been incorporated into Christ. Those who so live in union with Him as head, and with one another as members of His body form a community energized by His Spirit, and united in a family affinity of love.

Paul delighted in describing the fellowship of believers under such a figure. The record in Acts identifies him as a spectator at the martyrdom of Stephen (Acts 7:58,). Perhaps it was there (when Stephen's face reflected something of the glory of Jesus as he gazed into heaven [vv.55-56]) that the apostle-to-be first realized that Christ was alive in the lives of his followers. Certainly Stephen's patient suffering and forgiveness of his executioners (vv.59-60) showed him to be indwelt by the Spirit of Christ.

By the time of the Damascus road experience the pricks of conscience were strengthened by Jesus' claim that Paul was persecuting Him and not merely his followers. (Acts 26:14-15). From that moment on Paul no longer saw believers as the body of Christians but as the living body of Christ. (1 Cor.12:12-27, Rom.12:4,5).

The body metaphor refers primarily to our common dependence on Christ, joint partaking of His Spirit, unity in Him, and our interdependence and responsibility for mutual service to each other. And the analogy well suits the reality. A human body remains a unity although all of its members differ in form and function. We are each incomplete without all the others, and each is as significant and essential to the well being of the whole as any other.

We are incorporated into the body of Christ through the regeneration effected in each of us by the same Holy Spirit of Christ who now indwells us. (1 Cor.12:13). Our mutual recognition of belonging by faith to Christ brings an immediate sense of oneness with all His true people. On the general level this sense of unity transcends all time and denominational barriers. On the local level this leads to the desire to fellowship with those around us who share such a faith, and who express it in the manner which best accords with our own understandings of what it means to serve Him truly as Lord.

ONE BODY : GENERAL AND LOCAL

The New Testament speaks of the body of Christ as a Christian community first as a general, unseen, and eternal reality known only to God. But it then also uses the same term for any local, visible, and present expression of that unseen eternal reality as gathered in an earthly Christian assembly.

While we have abundant reference to the eternal body of Christ (Eph.1:22, 3:10,21, 5:23-32; Col.1:18,24; 1 Tim.3:15; Heb. 12:22-23.) 92 of the 115 times the word translated church or assembly (*ecclesia*) is used in the New Testament it appears to refer to a specific local assembly of believers gathered in fellowship in an earthly location. So the same image of the body is appropriate to describe any local gathered community of believers. Every local congregation reproduces Christ's body as each possesses many members with Him as head who relate to each other.

Confusion arises when we fail to realize that the figure of the church as Christ's body is applied in the Scriptures in this double manner. The ultimate entity of God's gathered people in eternity is described as the body — but so also are the individual earthly gatherings of the saints.

THE ETERNAL ASSEMBLY : HIS GENERAL BODY

The term "church" (literally "assembly") is often used in the Scriptures to identify the ultimate gathering in eternity composed of all the redeemed from all nations over all the ages of time who are spiritually born into a relationship with Christ and each other. (Eph.1:10, 3:6; Heb.12:22-23). It is this church whom Christ loved and for whom He died (Eph.5:2).

Thus we are told of the uniting power of salvation bringing Jews and Gentiles "both in one body to God through the cross..." (Eph.2:16). We also read of "the church of God "(Acts 20:8) which appears as something other than a mere geographical description like "the churches of Judea" (1 Thess.2:14) or "the churches of Galatia" (Gal.1:2). This concept arose from the common knowledge that all were one in body in Christ. It reveals a spiritual unity between all local assemblies of God's people, not an organizational one. 21 of the 27 books in the New Testament are apostolic letters written from leaders in one local assembly of Christians to others who together with all other believers in all ages make up the general body of Christ.

The whole family of God then resides in many locations, including the dead "in Christ", and the living among differing fellowships. If God is my Father then I have a family to whom I must relate in love. The various local churches were one in a united fellowship as illustrated by 1.Cor.12:13 where the apostle uses the collective "we" stating that both he and the Corinthians were baptized by the Spirit into that one body. But they were converted (and immersed in water for that matter) at Corinth, and he at Damascus. He also stated that both he and those participating in the Corinthian Christian assembly were members in "the body of Christ" while at the time of writing he was actively serving in association with the Christian assembly at Ephesus!

Writing to the Roman and Corinthian churches from Ephesus, and to the others in Galatia, Philippi, Thessalonica, and Ephesus

Paul saw them all as part of the one eternal body. He viewed them all as reflecting that same nature in their own local and visible characters. They found their real and essential unity in the eternal and invisible assembly of God.

This one body is also pictured in the New Testament by other various images. The church can be described biblically as one temple, one vine, one bride, one flock with many folds, and one household. So the pictures are all of unity. We are not one body alone at Corinth, another at Ephesus, others in Galatia. We are all one body in Christ, and our local visible assemblies reproduce that nature.

From such a perceived bonding Paul could speak of the Corinthian Christian's "duty" to give generously for support of the work in Jerusalem (1. Cor.16:1) in financial emergency. They discerned this unity because when one member suffers every member suffers with it (1 Cor.12:26). Acts 11:29 shows that the Antioch church (to which Paul belonged and where he ministered for years [Acts 13:1]), set the example for this kind of inter-assembly care long before when famine first threatened Judea.

This "body" must be described as eternal, universal, and as unseen by us as the identities and totality of all its members are known ultimately only to God. It is into this unseen and eternal assembly that we are "baptized" by the Holy Spirit — He alone makes us part of that body. (1 Cor.12:13).

(The majority of interpreters today see this 1 Cor. 12:13 reference as a description of the Spirit's work in regeneration and an underscoring of the part all believers have in that ultimate and eternal body. But some evangelicals [including an increasingly small number of Baptists] have struggled with this concept seeing the verse as referring to water baptism and as much a sacramental as a symbolic rite which brings the believer into the local assembly. They do not view water baptism as the confession that marks a person as a disciple, but consider that in some mystical manner such obedience actually makes the person a member of the local body. But if baptism automatically made one a "member" of the local body how could Paul, when first converted and baptized, be refused fellowship by the Jerusalem saints? Baptism alone was not enough. They also needed reliable testimony that his conversion was authentic from others before they would accept him. [Acts 9:19-31.].)

Down through their history Baptists have always advocated the idea of the local church as simply a geographically identifiable gathered community of believers who are first part of His body general by faith through regeneration by the Spirit. That history refers explicitly to the body of Christ as an eternal and universal church unseen as yet by us in its entirety — but fully known to God

Confessions of faith published by London Baptists (1644 & 1677) reflect such perspectives, as do the well known Philadelphia Confession (which reproduced the London 1677 materials in 1742), and the Charleston Baptist Association of South Carolina (1767) (which was an edition of the Philadelphia document). The New Hampshire Confession (1833) avoided any discussion of anything but what it termed "a Gospel Church" being the visible congregation of baptized believers. (Lumpkin, 1959:146, 285, 348, 352, 360.) The current SBC "Baptist Faith and Message" statement (1963) endorses the idea in article #7, as the chairman of its formulation committee expounds,

> *The church general, as composed of all the redeemed, is in the kingdom of God. The local church is an earthly colony of that kingdom. ...Each time a soul submits to God through Christ he enters the kingdom by willingly accepting God's rule. As such he becomes part of the church general. Through believer's baptism he becomes a part of the fellowship of the local church. ...Thus while salvation is synonymous with membership in the church general, it is not true with regard to local church membership. Nor is membership in the local church synonymous with salvation. "Fellowship" not "membership is the New Testament word for Christian relations in the local church. (Hobbs, 1971: 79-80)*

THE LOCAL ASSEMBLY: HIS BODY IN PARTICULAR

Each local grouping consists of believers who have identified their relationship with the eternal, universal, and general body by a confession of personal faith in Christ as Savior and Lord and by uniting with a temporary, local, and visible body of like-minded persons. Only within such a visible body can spiritual gifts be exercised and the individual members function so that they may grow and so that the eternal body can also be built up.

The visible church may be distinguished from the invisible as it is a society of professing believers organized for visible worship, proclamation, growth, and ministry. So we do not have many "bodies" of Christ but many local expressions of the one body of Christ each exhibiting many of the characteristics of the unseen reality.

A local church is the body of Christ in particular, as well as the whole church is His body in general. This is the exact truth Paul highlights when he talks of the body through 1.Cor.12:1-27. The whole chapter seems to discuss the church general, unseen, universal, and eternal.

But in verse 27 Paul changes the application of all said before to apply to the specific Corinthian assembly with the comment that as every one of them are members of Christ in particular so they are together a particular body of Christ.

Of course only God can judge just how much actual identity exists between a particular local assembly and the eternal congregation. All those who truly confess Jesus Christ as Lord in all the ages together comprise His eternal body.

Baptists endeavor to ensure what local reality they can by requiring a personal confession through voluntary baptism before admitting those who claim faith into their local fellowships. But of course no requirement, even this one, can absolutely guarantee the reality of an individual's faith. Many will truly be God's children also in other communions, and some will belong to none, if the criterion for acceptance in the eternal family of God is simple faith in Christ as Lord and Savior. The parable of the wheat and tares should encourage us to leave all such final judgments in the Lord's hands.

2. A GLORIOUS CHURCH

When Paul affirms that there is one body and one Spirit he continues reminding us also that "you were called in one hope of your calling" (Eph.4:4). The calling to which Paul refers is the assurance that the imperfect visible body of Christ on earth will ultimately become the perfect body of Christ in eternity, no longer invisible, but now matured "to the measure of the stature which belongs to the fullness of Christ". (v.13).

Thus in Eph. 5 he talks of the entire eternal assembly who Jesus loved and for whom He gave His life (v.25) and asserts the purpose of his sacrifice to be the complete cleansing of His people

> ... that He might present to Himself the church in all her glory, having no spot or wrinkle or any such thing: but that she should be holy and blameless. (Eph.5:27)

In Christ God established a new order of creation with Him as its Head. The church will finally be perfected as one universal assembly in eternity as part of God's plan for a restored universe, with Christ as the focal center for this restoration.

The apostle knew part of this great mystery to be the fact that "... the Gentiles are fellow-heirs and fellow-members of the body, and fellow-partakers of the promise in Christ Jesus ..." (Eph. 3:6). He saw our salvation by grace as the revelation of His will that His intention was lead the present body of Christ to such a fullness of glory. (Eph. 1:6-10).

This is the hope which can only be described as a certain inheritance of which the presence of the Holy Spirit in our hearts is the pledge. (Eph. 1:11-14).

3. MEANS FOR MATURITY

Accordingly he describes God's present gifts of ministry to the church as including pastor-teachers "for the equipping of the saints for the work of service, to the building up of the body of Christ;" (Eph. 4:12) God does not gift the church with leaders to lift the load of service from the shoulders of others. Gifted leaders exist to equip others to function more effectively in their own work.

The word translated "equip" (*katartismon*) means a work of restoration to useful service. Matthew uses the same verb (4:21) where Jesus discovers James and John "mending", or "perfecting" their nets. In other places the same word speaks of restoring those overtaken in a fault, and as the way God works with others as part of our mutual responsibility to all members in the body. (Gal.6:1, 2 Cor.13:11, Heb.13:21, 1 Pet.5:10).

Present gifts within the church therefore facilitate personal spiritual growth and the upbuilding of the body through mutual ministry. The final objective is stated as that ultimate total unity of faith and knowledge that is full maturity — the perfection which is "... the measure of the stature which belongs to the fullness of Christ". (Eph.4:13).

God's ultimate plan calls for our complete conformity to Jesus Christ. His body, not yet perfect, is to grow increasingly toward that eternal ideal. Where local leaders minister effectively equipping others for their own ministries the present body increases in strength, power, and maturity. And therefore,

> *As a result we are no longer to be children, tossed here and there by waves, and carried about by every wind of doctrine, by the trickery of men, by craftiness in deceitful scheming; but speaking the truth in love, we are to grow up in all aspects into Him, who is the head, even Christ... (Eph.4:14-15).*

The immediate intention for Christ's body as we find it expressed locally on earth is to equip its members for more effective functioning. The ultimate intention for Christ's body is that we be as fully perfect in eternity as He is Himself.

Thus the present body grows gradually towards maturity. Christlikeness, spiritual stability and the practice of truth spoken in love evidence our growth towards the ultimate goal of a fullness in the body which corresponds with the fullness of its head. This final perfection can only be realized in eternity when every member has reached his or her full stature. But our present growth as body members linked with others through Christ is also a dynamic which can unify and enable all to move toward that ultimate fullness.

In Eph.4:16 we see present members of the body bracing each other, adjusting to each other, linking up as channels of power and grace flowing from Christ, and helping the whole body to grow towards that future full maturity.

4. THE EVANGELICAL HERITAGE

The term "Evangelical" is a good biblically based word arising from the Greek word used most often in the Scriptures to describe the open proclamation of the good news of the Gospel of grace through the atonement effected by Christ. It affirms a theology that centers on the personal experience of conversion.

In his volume marking the twenty-fifth anniversary of the *American National Association of Evangelicals* Shelley defined evangelicals as

> *...Christians who are concerned with that personal experience of Christ that results from the preaching of the Biblical gospel. Evangelicals are "orthodox" Christians in the sense that they accept the cardinal doctrines of historic Protestantism, but they are convinced that the true doctrine of Christ must be followed by a true decision for Christ. (Shelley, 1967: 7-8).*

The standard understanding of an "evangelical church" is

> *... especially, any of certain Protestant churches that stress the preaching of the gospel of Jesus Christ, personal conversion experiences, Scripture as the only basis for faith, and active home and foreign evangelism. (New Encyclopedia Britannica, Vol. 1. 1986:613).*

The word "Evangelical" has been applied historically in many contexts but, as it is best used today, it emphasizes natural man's need for a spiritual rebirth through a response of faith to God's invitation of forgiveness provided through the atonement effected by the death of Christ. Evangelicals hold that conversion is an individual and profound experience, generated by the Holy Spirit and resulting in a life-commitment to Jesus as Lord.

> *In simplest terms an evangelical is a Christian who accepts and lives the gospel... Evangelicalism ...emphasizes man's need for a spiritual rebirth*

in the experience of conversion... (they) insist
that Christianity is more than theological
orthodoxy and religious conservativism. It is a
spirit, a concern for sinners, a way of life. Its
master motif is the salvation of souls: its guiding
image the redemptive gospel of Jesus Christ. All
other considerations are subordinated to this
standard. (Shelley, 1967:15-17).

The realization of such a vitality may arise dramatically as it did with Saul of Tarsus on the road to Damascus, or through the witness of a faithful family context as it did with young Timothy. The experience may vary (and its specificity even be unfocused) but the reality of that new life depending solely on God's Grace in Christ must be cardinal.

The best proof that a natural birth did occur is found in an animated person living vitally before others, and not in some paper certifying the time and place of a birth. In the same manner an authentic faith reveals its reality best through the evidence of a vital spiritual life in the present even where the details of spiritual birth cannot be documented.

Reverence for the authority of the Scriptures and a passion to spread the good news of the gospel through evangelism and missions seem to arise as natural outcomes from such an experience.

An evangelical line can be traced from the Puritanism of the reformers in the Church of England and Anglican leaders such as John Newton, to the English Evangelical revival of the eighteenth century. This movement rejuvenated all English-speaking Christianity mainly under the leadership of John and Charles Wesley and George Whitefield. The influence of European Pietistic and Moravian movements, and evangelical leaders of social conscience such as William Wilberforce and Lord Shaftsbury, joined with evangelical noncomformity, represented by preachers such as C.H. Spurgeon, to lead to today's situation.

American Evangelicalism still owes much to its English roots building on the Great Awakening revival in the North. This began in the 1720s and exploded from 1740 to 1742 in New England under the ministry of the same George Whitefield who had been so active in the English movement. (Shelley, 1967: 7-67; Ewell, 1984:379-382).

I have written in detail elsewhere of the subsequent history of Evangelicalism and Fundamentalism. I have also documented there how the latter began as a mainstream evangelical movement but subsequently degenerated into an iconoclastic aberration of its original character. (Skinner, 1984: 204-213)

In a recent volume in which two Baptist scholars debated whether Southern Baptists were Evangelicals or not the editor found the question open and unresolved. One scholar believed in the equation and affirmed that Southern Baptists do

> *...exemplify the great heritage of Scriptural authority, Christocentric doctrine, gospel proclamation, experience of grace, and evangelistic endeavor which is Evangelicalism. (Garrett, 1983: 126).*

His protagonist saw Baptist identity as including an evangelical element but as centering historically on the concept of faith as a free and voluntary exercise of the individual. From such a principle he insisted that the Baptist vigilance for religious liberty and separation of church and state arose. (Garrett, 1983:147).

But the first scholar defined Evangelicalism as a term covering many groups with the common core of belief as in the above quotation. The second man saw it as a movement characterized mostly by a fighting fundamentalist mentality.

Obviously if we reframe that question as "Is the present Southern Baptist character indebted to the Evangelical heritage more than any other" a more affirmative answer is readily possible.

A Lesson From History

Historically Baptists refused to be religiously coerced and suffered persecution for their principles of individual liberty. But those among them, who (with some Congregationalists) turned aside from an evangelical theological core of belief to emphasize such principles *alone*, became the founders of the Unitarian and Universalist churches with their non-biblical character. For those who refused such an eclectic compromise Evangelicalism remains as the most spiritual element of our present heritage, and as the pervasive factor which most characterizes our common Baptist worship and ministries today.

Baptist historians generally concede that the First Baptist Church of Charleston, South Carolina, organized the first Baptist church in the South there in the late seventeenth century. Their emphases included a strong commitment to local church autonomy and independence. Leaders such as William Screven, Oliver Hart, and Richard Furman enlarged this tradition through their work in the local Baptist association with a focus on a sophisticated approach to worship and church order.

Other streams which flowed into the Southern Baptist heritage include the Georgia tradition with its sense of Southern pride, co-operative Christian endeavor, and zeal for missions, and the Tennessee tradition (often termed "Landmarkism") which emphasized a separation from other Christians and a pride in that exclusivism. (Shurden, 1981).

But the most formative factor, in terms of present-day Southern Baptist identity, arose from the churches of the Separate Baptists of the South. Only three years after they had migrated from New England to Sandy Creek, North Carolina, Daniel Marshall and Shubal Stearns founded the Sandy Creek Baptist Association in 1758. In a day when only 47 Baptist churches existed in the entire nation (and only 7 of these were anywhere in the South) these two pioneer Baptists established another 42 churches and ordained 25 preachers in only 17 years. (Lumpkin, 1961, Shurden, 1981). Their powerful ministry began an evangelistic, revivalistic, and highly biblical programs and tradition of church growth and outreach which still continues today across the entire Southern Baptist Convention as its most obvious characteristic.

And these two men found their powerful faith through the "Great Awakening", the major Northern evangelistic movement stimulated by George Whitfield associate of John and Charles Wesley in the great English Evangelical Revival. (Lumpkin, 1961). This same English awakening also brought the modern missions movement to birth through Baptist pastor, William Carey. The Wesleys founded Methodism, Whitfield served as an

Independent, but all, including Marshall and Stearns, were staunch Evangelicals.

Lumpkin (1961) unhesitatingly affirms that these "Separate Baptists" who were the revivalists of the "Great Awakening in the South" (p.147) helped establish the character of aggressive American Christianity and lie as roots to the Baptist concepts of voluntaryism, democracy, and denominationalism (p.148). They largely provided leadership for the American frontier, provided a moral and spiritual base for the erection of the American democratic revolution and the struggle for liberty, and contributed in many other cardinal ways to the strength of religious faith today. (pp.148-150). He asserts,

> *In many distinguishable ways the Separate Baptists live on in Southern Baptists. Most notable is the general spirit and outlook of the Southern Baptist people. (Lumpkin, 1961:158).*

He continues citing the evangelism and missions consciousness of Baptist in the South as facilitating their amazing growth compared with American (Northern) Baptists who lacked this "evangelical" spirit. He also demonstrates how the autonomy of the local church, reflected in the Southern convention structures, the focus on a public professions of faith leading to baptism and church membership, and the commitment to lay leadership all reflect some of these perspectives. (Ibid:159-162).

> *...the Separate Baptist movement ...infused such life into the Baptist denomination in America as to raise it from obscurity to prominence within a quarter of a century. By reason of this brief history it made Baptists the principal beneficiaries in America of the Great Awakening. (Ibid:162).*

This analysis is confirmed by modern historians outside of SBC who claim our that we exist as "the largest distinctively evangelical denomination in the United States" (Quebedeaux, 1978:36).

We are also regarded by such authorities as displaying unusual openness to new ideas and more inclusivist in our membership and ministries that some other evangelicals. (*Ibid*:38).

An English Baptist scholar pinpoints adherence to the ordinances as a major reason for this evangelical focus, discussing the cumulative effect of continually "showing forth the Lord's death" to His church around the table and to the world through the believer's immersion.

> *The cumulative effect of this repetition, even from a purely psychological point of view, must be very great. To this must be ascribed the general continuity of "evangelicalism" within the Baptist community. They are repeatedly brought face to face with the facts of the death and resurrection of Jesus Christ as the salient articles of their faith... (Robinson, 1946:80; Cf.:147).*

A further confirmation of the significance of our evangelical heritage as Southern Baptists is the realization that our hymnal collections would be in tatters if we excised all evangelical writers from its pages. When Broadman Press editors researched over 30,000 churches for the 1975 Baptist hymnal to see what our people sang and preferred, evangelical themes dominated.

Their collection includes Isaac Watts' 16 hymns (Independent) which match our own B. B. McKinney as the most in that publication. Charles Wesley (Methodist) comes closest to these among all the others with 12 of his hymns included.

Southern Baptists still love to sing "Blessed Assurance" and "To God Be The Glory" by Fanny Crosby (Methodist), "What a Friend We Have In Jesus" by Joseph Scriven (Plymouth Brethren), "I Will Sing of My Redeemer" by P. P. Bliss (Congregationalist), "Jesus Calls Us Oe'r the Tumult" by Mrs. C. F. Alexander (Anglican), "Rock of Ages" by A. M. Toplady (Anglican), "Faith is The Victory" and "Simply Trusting Ev'ry Day" by Ira D. Sankey (Methodist), and "Amazing Grace" by John Newton (Anglican). The one commonality which binds all these together, and with many other of our hymnal contributors, is that they were all known in their day as "Evangelicals".

"Wonderful, Wonderful Jesus" (E.O. Sellers); "Take Time to Be Holy", "Jesus Is Calling" (George C. Stebbins); "Great is Thy Faithfulness" (William M. Runyan); "Make Me a Blessing" (George S. Schuler); "Trust and Obey", and "Grace That Is Greater Than All Our Sin" (Daniel B. Towner); are also all included in the hymnal. All of the above five composers spent a large portion of their lives associated with the Moody Bible Institute in Chicago, a major center of Evangelical life and ministry. (Flood, 1987).

Contemporaries who continue to influence Southern Baptists musically today include John Peterson, who contributed "So Send I You", "Surely Goodness and Mercy", and "Heaven Came Down" to our hymnal. He also came from Moody. One of Southern Baptist Seminary's present senior professors of music, Dr. Don Hustad, taught on the faculty of Moody, and served later at the very heart of evangelical life through his participation as organist and staff musician with the Billy Graham Evangelistic Association.

As this material was being prepared Southern Baptists has just completed intensive analyses of current hymn usage from the 1975 Baptist Hymnal. They selected 200 of the most frequently used hymns for inclusion in the new hymnal published in 1991. The 126 page research report published by the Baptist Sunday School Board revealed the following to be the "top ten" in frequency of usage, and that all were distinctly of the evangelical "gospel song" type of hymn.

> 1. *Amazing Grace*
> 2. *To God Be the Glory*
> 3. *Victory in Jesus*
> 4. *Just As I Am*
> 5. *Blessed Assurance*
> 6. *Standing on the Promises*
> 7. *Have Thine Own Way, Lord*
> 8. *Power In the Blood*
> 9. *At the Cross*
> 10. *At Calvary*
>
> *(Anderson, 1988:19-32)*

The first 50 hymns in popularity were also actually of this

same flavor! (See note at end of this chapter; p. 66.)*

Our Baptist heritage also includes such illustrious evangelicals as William Carey, Alexander McLaren, F.B. Meyer, Charles Haddon Spurgeon and Billy Graham, and many others. In the course of my present ministry I visit dozens of churches each year. I never find a pastor's library composed only of publications written by Baptists. The bulk of our pastors' libraries consist almost entirely of volumes by evangelical publishers prepared by authors from every conceivable denomination. So historically, musically, and in terms of the resources on which we mostly draw for our practical theology, ministry, and preaching, we are still influenced by the evangelical heritage more than any other.

Of course we cannot equate the Southern Baptist movement with Evangelicalism but we cannot deny this heritage nor its significance as larger than any other on our present day Baptist life. The fullness of Southern Baptists distinctives is more than can be contained in such a word but no other movement in history has contributed more to what we are than has this one.

Even that sector of Evangelicalism which is most conservative (and which clusters with its independent and "Bible" churches around what can be described as the "Dallas Seminary/ Moody Bible Institute Axis") displays surprisingly "Baptistic" doctrines and practices. The denominational theology and program which most "interdenominationalists" of today display seems to be closest to a Southern Baptist ethos than to almost anything else.

Pigeon holes may be fine for pigeons but persons do not fit into them very well. Yet, as our human capacity to understand seems so often to depend upon classification and identification, we try constantly to force others into the pre-conceived shapes we have chosen for them. Labels so easily become libels because their use reveals as much about the user as it does about those being designated. Like worn coins poplar words lose their clarity when over-used.

Thus, when we call persons "conservative" from a positive perspective the name can highlight their adherence to time tested values. Such a person may feel deeply and commendably that thoughtless change can too easily destroy essential and foundational elements fundamental to the issues concerned.

Likewise, when we call persons "progressive" from a positive perspective, we may be viewing them as those who are very favorable to constructive change, and worthy of approval because of their open-mindedness.

But we may also consider someone to be "conservative" from a negative perspective. We can regard that person to be so threatened by the growth and adjustment potentials which any rational change demands that he or cannot progress at all. We can also describe others as "progressive" from a negative perspective. By this we can mean that we view them as so uncommitted to any absolutes, and so broad-minded that the desire for anxiety to change retards all objective judgment. Thus the terms we use often import unconscious distortions into their definitions. They seldom express crystal clear objective realities.

In reality the church has always had to balance the progressive against the conservative in its life and history. Had we lacked commitment to the biblical fundamentals of faith we would long since have deserted the evangelical doctrines. Had we not been progressive we would still be struggling musically in our worship with poorly-rhymed psalms, and singing *a capella* without any instrumental supports or hymn books as our great grandfathers tried to do.

Almost 40 years ago the editors of *Look* magazine posed a question to a young Baptist evangelist about to lead a large crusade in New York. When they asked if he was fundamentalist or liberal in theology Billy Graham replied —

> ... *if by fundamentalist you mean "narrow", "bigoted", "prejudiced," "extremist," "emotional," "snake handler", "without social conscience"* — *then I am definitely not a fundamentalist.*
> *However if by fundamentalist you mean a person who accepts the authority of the Scriptures, the virgin birth of Christ, the atoning death of Christ, His bodily resurrection, His second coming and personal salvation by faith through grace, then I am a fundamentalist. However I much prefer being called a "Christian". The terms liberalism and fundamentalism have arisen in modern days.*

Neither is found in sacred scripture. ("Billy Graham...", 1956: 49).

The evangelical fundamentalists who group themselves with Rev. Jerry Falwell have, in the past, been seen as militant and divisive. In recent days, however, their spokesmen appear to be recognizing some of the dangers of such extremist positions. Edward Dobson recently presented two *Fundamentalist Journal* editorials adapted from his volume *In Search of Unity* (1985). In the first he listed such fundamentalist strengths as a militant commitment to the truth revealed in Scripture which adherence leads to an aggressive preaching ministry and evangelistic programming, and to a strong directive leadership in local pastorates. He affirmed some major values of evangelicals to be the control that keeps them from slipping into extremist postures, their practical emphasis on love and hesitancy to judge others, and their emphases on biblical teaching and exposition, worship and scholarship. (Dobson, 1957a).

In his second editorial in the *Fundamentalist Journal* Dobson called for a clear rejection of some extremisms offered by both fundamentalists and evangelicals. He very courageously analyzed fundamentalist's weaknesses by defining them as often intolerant, hasty in their judgments, inflexible to constructive change, over proud of their achievements, intimidated by others evaluations of them, and tending to such separation from mainstream Christianity that they become almost isolated. In the same article Dobson defines evangelical weaknesses as including such a moderation that they were sometimes over tolerant and allowed error to continue unchecked. He also found evangelicals often to be so intellectually proud that their theology lacked substance, and (by their over concern for academic and social respectability) often so open to compromise that "...the left wing of Evangelicalism is barely discernable from the right wing of Liberalism". (Dobson, 1957b).

Such comments come from within the ranks of the far right of conservative belief. They appear to show at least some potential for the development of a coming balance without bias. Certainly the weaknesses of both movements can be ameliorated by a joint rejection of such extremes.

5. AFFINITY NOT ENTITY

The insights which arise from an understanding of the church as the body of Christ is that we need a working relationship with other members of that body on earth based on a familial relationship. Those who are Christ's should find a unity together based on their common spiritual birth into God's family and their common calling to move toward a destiny of perfection. Within this unity variety seems essential. Eyes, hands, mouth, and feet all remain distinctive within the body but they all belong together and thus are interdependent. We belong to each other, and we need each other, so we must care for each other, and balance each other. The high priestly prayer of Jesus asks for just such a unity within diversity, a unity modelled on the intimate fellowship of distinctive personalities within the Godhead, "...that they may be one even as we are" (John 17:11). This was not a prayer for the creation of an entity related by sameness but for the building of a unity which welded their togetherness through love without denying individuality.

The unity of the Spirit arises as an intuitive and affective assurance enabling us to discern others who are truly born of Him. This reality bonds us one to another in Christ. Because we share this same fundamental inward experience this is a tie that can bind us together in fellowship without exact correspondence in other matters. Some see unity erroneously as a kind of monolithic sameness in which individuals lose identity but the Bible sees it as fellowship within the family. So the church cannot be a monolithic entity, like a solid slab of granite, dense and immobile. It must flow more like a family fellowship whose linkage needs continual renewal and whose reproduction adds continually to its numbers and nature. The church must be a living organism. It requires a continual and disciplined effort in order to maintain each part in suitable relationship so that it nourishes life and encourages growth. True Christian brotherhood and sisterhood arises through the affinitive relationships of children born from the same Father who live supremely for the family's interests above their own. The whole family fellowship is much larger than any particular element within it. The insight which discerns an affinity between all the members of the family in relationship is the catalyst which makes all the other parts work effectively.

Because of the fraternal relationship between its members a family maintains its fellowship by making many allowances, forgiving failures, and by restoring those who struggle. No family is an entity with each participant an exact replica of the other. The family hangs together because of its affinity — the quality of oneness born from a common parentage and the shared relationships which arise therefrom. Affinity among a family does not then demand a levelling uniformity but rather fosters an authentic harmony based on mutual esteem. Family fellowship, produces a mutuality of affection in distinction to mere mechanical organization which only builds a sterile conformity. As with any family real unity can only exist within God's household as the fraternal affinity is preserved by its members.

Unity among the children of God may best be described as "a working relationship of acceptance without total entity". This intuitive and affective assurance of oneness is real at levels beneath and beyond mere mechanical and surface association. It exists as a matter of the heart, the mind, and the will. It is a spirit and insight felt and caught rather than merely something to be argued or taught.

Because you belong to Christ
You are akin to me,
One in the bonds unbreakable,
Wrought for eternity.
Spirit with spirit joined,
Who can these ties undo,
Binding the Christ within my heart
Unto the Christ in you ?
— anonymous lines from an old
Autograph Book

NOTE

* The 40 most used hymns in Southern Baptist churches (after the "top 10" mentioned earlier in this chapter) as ranked by official B.S.S.B. research survey March, 1988, are listed below. Note that these, too are all of the "evangelical gospel song" type and that the choice of classic worship and praise hymns is minimal. The same preferences continue through the entire ranking of 512 levels and it is not until around the 50 mark that the Christmas carols and other standard worship hymns one would expect to be in evidence start to appear.

11. He Keeps Me Singing
12. Only Trust Him
13. Softly and Tenderly
14. Love Lifted Me
15. How Great Thou Art
16. He Lives
17. Leaning on the Everlasting Arms
18. There Is a Name I Love to Hear
19. Jesus is Tenderly Calling Thee Home
20. Praise Him! Praise Him!
21. 'Tis so Sweet to Trust in Jesus
22. Down At the Cross
23. Nothing But the Blood
24. Trust and Obey
25. The Solid Rock
26. Count Your Blessings
27. Are You Washed in the Blood?
28. I Surrender All
29. The Old Rugged Cross
30. Footsteps of Jesus
31. I Am Thine O Lord
32. Because He Lives
33. I Have Decided to Follow Jesus
34. What a Friend We Have in Jesus
35. When We All Get to Heaven
36. Showers of Blessing
37. Take Up Thy Cross and Follow Me
38. Since Jesus Came Into My Heart
39. I Stand Amazed in the Presence
40. I Love to Tell the Story
41. Jesus Saves
42. Jesus Paid It All
43. Revive Us Again
44. Stand Up for Jesus
45. Higher Ground
46. Living for Jesus
47. I Will Sing the Wond'rous Story
48. When the Roll Is Called up Yonder
49. Take the Name of Jesus with You
50. Sweet, Sweet Spirit.

(Anderson, 1988:19-32)

5 ....*one Lord, one faith, one baptism,*
6. *one God and Father of all who is over all and through all and in all*

— Ephesians 4

1. *See how great a love the Father has bestowed upon us that we should be called children of God; and such we are. For this reason the world does not know us, because it did not know Him.*
2. *Beloved, now are we the children of God, and it has not appeared as yet what we shall be. We know that, when He appears, we hall be like Him, because we shall see Him just as He is*

— 1 John 3

7. *For many deceivers have gone out into the world, those who do not acknowledge Jesus Christ as coming in the flesh. This is the deceiver and the antichrist.*
9. *Any one who goes too far and does not abide in the teaching of Christ, does not have God; the one who abides in the teaching, he has both the Father and the Son.*
10. *If any one comes to you and does not bring this teaching, do not receive him into your house, and do not give him a greeting;*
11. *for the one who gives him a greeting participates in his evil deeds*

— 11 John

❦

Dynamic Three: Focus

The Doctrinal Tie — Centrality Not Identity

I would propose that the subject of the ministry in this house, as long as this platform shall stand, and as long as this house shall be frequented by worshippers, shall be the person of JESUS CHRIST. I am never ashamed to avow myself a Calvinist, I do not hesitate to take the name of Baptist; but if I am asked what is my creed, I reply, "It is Jesus Christ". My venerated predecessor, Dr. Gill, has left a 'Body of Divinity'* admirable and excellent in its way, but the 'Body of Divinity' to which I would pin and bind myself for ever, God helping me, is not his system, or any other human treatise; but Christ Jesus, who is the sum and substance of the Gospel, who is in Himself all theology, the incarnation of every precious truth, the all glorious personal embodiment of the Way, the Truth, and the Life.

— C.H. Spurgeon's first words in the Metropolitan Tabernacle, London, 1861

---

*- an allusion to Gill's heavy volumes on theology

1. THE DOCTRINAL TIE

We have examined the spiritual tie of unity (expressed as an attitude that strives to keep the bond of peace), and the family tie of affinity (expressed through a mutuality between all who truly belong to the body of Christ). But neither of these can function best to bind us together in effective cooperation without some common basic beliefs.

What is the nature of this shared doctrinal focus? How can we facilitate its function as an energizing catalyst to accelerate spiritual momentum? In what manner does it relate to the differing local, denominational, and transdenominational levels of Christian fellowship? How does it function positively to validate the proper (and often distinctive) confessions of faith which we all agree do have value for our churches and other co-operative Christian associations?

Christians in the past fashioned doctrinal agreements and confessions as a way of expressing shared beliefs. Unfortunately they sometimes they used these confessional documents as creeds by which to endeavor to force unity. Such confessions of faith expressed by any earthly society of believers possess real value whether they come from a local Christian assembly, or from individuals or whole assemblies in fellowship as denominations, or even across such lines.

Confessions may well articulate our shared beliefs and mark differences of biblical interpretation which clarify special concerns and distinguish those groups and individuals from others who also belong to Christ. But a philosophy of spiritual association which limits our fellowship only to one among those Christians who totally identify with our confessions in every minute detail is unworkable and foreign to the New Testament.

Identity between believers in all things awaits our release from the human condition and our transformation into total conformity to Christ in the eternal state. John affirms that by God's grace we now are called the children of God, but although this is our true nature it is by no means our present state. Only when we finally view Him as He truly is in eternal glory shall we also display the full reality of our own nature as objectively identified with Him. (1 John 3:1-3).

In our state of present existence we only see Jesus as He *was*. As He was in Bethlehem, as He was in Galilee, as He was in

Jerusalem, as He was at Calvary, and as He was at the resurrection. This is a limited vision and only a dim picture of His real glory and we see it as a poor image reflected in the pages of the Scriptures. One day we shall see Him as He truly *is*! When our earthly faith vision resolves finally into an unrestricted sight vision of His face-to-face glory we shall know fully instead of in part. (1 Cor. 13: 9-12).

Paul highlights the ridiculousness of an identity of every member in the body now with some satirical questions directed to the early Christians.

> *If the whole body were an eye where would the hearing be? If the whole were hearing where would the sense of smell be? (1 Cor. 12:17).*

It only takes a moment to picture how horribly distorted a human body would be if it all were an ear, or all were a nose, and to see how such a body would be a monstrosity and could not live without individuality in its members. Until we are all like Christ each functions as an individual as diverse, yet as unified, as every body is under its head. We shall not lose that individuality in the glorious church yet finally to be revealed, but, because we are transformed into His likeness we shall then be all identical in strength, in power to function, and in fullness of understanding and belief. Until then we remain diverse.

Despite all our efforts, we cannot seem to achieve a total present identity of doctrine. This is because such a unity awaits our entrance into the eternal state of absolute conformity to Christ. How then can we rationally demand such a stringent uniformity of doctrine to be a practical test of fellowship while here below?

The apostle asserts that our unity in the body builds upon the realities of "one Lord" and, "one faith". (Eph. 4:5a). For him the irreducible core of essential doctrine is the Christological — the Person of Christ, and the soteriological — His Work in providing salvation. He believed that the reality of Christ as the incarnate Son of God, who "loved the church and gave Himself up for her" (Eph.5:25), was the one fundamental foundation upon which the unity of the body could be built.

Yet some today appear to hold that only either a conservative or a progressive view of the process of biblical inspiration can be a satisfactory nucleus for true spiritual unity. If so proponents of both views seem to be at variance with Paul. He insists that the one, primary, and essential need for the cultivation of the fellowship and unity of the body is a sharpened focus on the Person and Work of Jesus Christ. He must be exalted as the Son of God through whose effective atonement for sin we are justified by faith as fellow believers in one body. "Jesus Christ is Lord" remains as the primary core for all Christian fellowship, in the local church, and at denominational or transdenominational levels.

2. FOCUS ON THE PERSON

Was Jesus Christ merely a man? A great man, perhaps the greatest man who ever lived, or was He, indeed, the eternal Son of God revealed in human flesh? This is a critical question, central and fundamental to faith, which cannot be bypassed. Christ was born, grew, lived suffered and died as many other men have, but was He also God? If He was not God in human flesh we are left merely with a religion of great words, attractive ideas and compelling ethics. But if He truly was God Christianity remains unique, not as a discovery made by men, but as a revelation given to men.

The angels announced Him to be "the Lord" at His birth (Luke 2:11). His Father acknowledged this at His baptism. (Matt. 3:16-17. The early converts confessed it (Acts 8:37). Paul asserted it (Rom. 9:5) and taught that His exaltation would demand the bending of every knee before His Majesty in eternity, and a confession from every tongue about His Lordship. (Phil. 2:8-11).

If Christ be not God He is the supreme imposter of the ages, a deceiver unworthy of being followed or revered. Again and again He claimed to be such, and demonstrated it by many signs, and wonders. Never man spake as He and never man lived as He. No explanation for the power and courage of His disciples, and for the amazing spread of the early Church after His cross, has ever been satisfactorily offered other than the simple reality the Scriptures share that they knew Him to be truly the Son of God, raised from the dead, and ascended to His Father.

The word "Lord" was used by His disciples not merely as a synonym for "master" or "sir" but as the equivalent of the Old Testament "Jehovah". He accepted the title (John 13:13, 20:28) and the New Testament applies the Old Testament titles of God to Him such as the "Lord of glory", the "Lord of Hosts" etc. In one explicit passage John explains that the "Jehovah, lofty and exalted" whom the prophet saw (Isaiah 6:1-4) was actually a vision of Jesus. (John 12:41).

The New Testament sees Christ as the divine agent in creation, the predestined Lord of the universe, and the exact representation of the Father. (Heb. 1:1-3). Writing to the Christians at Colosse Paul reveals his understanding of Christ as Creator and Sustained of the universe, and of His destiny to be the pre-eminent One in eternity. (Col. 1:15-18, 2:9).

No man or woman does violence to intellect to believe Him to be God. An objective examination of the bold claims of Jesus, his flawless character (testified to even by his opponents), and of the records written by eyewitnesses, sustains this conviction. The New Testament documents can be clearly affirmed as recording the facts as those who wrote them observed them, and have been so sustained on the rules of evidence alone when some have challenged them in several court cases. Ample collations confirming these proofs are readily available which set out this evidence in uncomplicated forms. (Cf. Stott, 1958; Walvoord, 1969).

The second and third epistles of John create a contrast illustrating how love always takes precedence above doctrine except in this one particular issue. In III John he writes to a church troubled by the problem of fellowship. He commends them for their reception of brethren whom they do not know but who share faith in Christ as Lord. (vv.3-8).

He discusses the relationship of truth to love (vv.9-10) by dealing with a power hungry brother, named Diotrephes, in the assembly who seeks to close off fellowship and eject any who do not follow his own particular twisted interpretations of doctrine. The apostle contrasts Diotrephes' judgmental attitudes and false beliefs with those of the good Demetrius. (vv.9-12). John's counsel is to retain fellowship with the one who does not even accept the teachings that the apostle himself offers because of the oneness and unity between all members of the body who share faith.

Love is always therefore larger than truth except in the one other special instance which John explains in II John, 7-8. Here he firmly teaches that no fellowship is possible with those who do not confess that Christ is God in the flesh and who departs from this understanding of His Person. His advice on separation on this ground even extends to avoiding discussions and not inviting them into our homes. (vv.9-10). (This seems to be very practical advice for some Christians, troubled today as to how they should relate to Jehovah's Witnesses, Mormons, and other cults who reject the deity of Christ. A brief word of testimony to such followed by dismissal would seem to be the appropriate scriptural counsel.)

THE VIRGIN BIRTH

Over many years one intellectual rationale for the affirmation of Christ's deity has been the biblical teaching about His "virgin birth". The accounts in Luke appear to have come from Mary and other eyewitnesses, and those in Matthew are given as fulfillments of Old Testament promises. Just because the clear accounts appear only on these two pages of the New Testament is no reason for rejection. If that were so, we should also have to reject the Sermon on the Mount as spurious for its records appear in exactly the same measure and by exactly the same authors!

Paul and others do make allusions to the truth (Gal. 4:4, 1 Tim. 3:16). But belief in the virgin birth, while it builds a logical rationale for faith, is not a requirement for salvation — faith in the deity of Christ is the requirement; faith that the value of the sinless life laid down is an effective sacrifice to atone for human sin.

How a person arrives at such a belief is quite secondary to the fact itself. I, personally, cannot conceive of a rationale which supports that deity which does not include the virgin birth. But I must allow for the right of another to hold a proper biblical view, by faith, of the Person and Work of Christ, without having to reach such a conclusion only in the manner in which I have reached it.

The virgin birth is a clear teaching of the Scriptures (and I personally have no doubts whatever about its truth) but our faith is to be placed in the reality of His deity, *and not in any particular rationale for it.*

74

If we involve the virgin birth as a fundamental requirement for salvation I, and many others are lost for I received Christ by faith at the age of 12 — when I was not even sure what a virgin was, let alone could believe intelligently in that doctrine! What we hold is important not why.

No evidence of the teaching of this concept exists with the Philippian jailor, the Ethiopian eunuch, the dying thief, or of a multitude of other convert whose stories are listed in the Scriptures. They certainly may have come to understand this truth as they lived for Christ, but simple faith in 'Jesus Christ as Lord' with all the assurance of justification by faith through his atonement and resurrection which such a belief implies, is the only criterion for salvation and for fellowship with other believers.

3. FOCUS ON THE WORK

Once we accept the deity of Christ we then must consider the purpose for which He became a participant in the human experience. The Gospels and the Epistles all affirm that He came into the world "to seek and save that which was lost". (Luke 19:10). Again many simple collations set out the evidence supporting coming to be the Savior who would lay down His sinless life as a substitute for ours, and open up a way for our forgiveness are readily available. (Cf. Stott, 1958; Walvoord, 1969).

Writing to the Corinthians Paul said that the reality of his resurrection is a foundation for our belief in His Deity (1. Cor. 15). He reminded the Romans that Jesus was "declared to be the Son of God with power by the resurrection from the dead". (Rom. 1:4). Peter also declared that the resurrection proved His Deity (Acts 2:36). In his clearest confessional passage Paul asserts that confession of Jesus as Lord, and belief with the heart that God raised Him from the dead, together evidence the reality of faith and provide the only certain path to salvation. (Rom. 10:9).

The one fundamental doctrinal tie which binds believers together is the one Lord, and the one faith in the meaning of His life, death and resurrection for our salvation. Thus the focus of the one faith falls clearly on both the Person and the Work of Christ.

This "one faith" of which the apostle speaks is not a total system of doctrine but rather the shared common experience of Jesus as Savior and Lord which provides the centrality for our trust. The ultimate identity and "unity of faith" in all things awaits our complete and eternal maturity in the fulness of Christ yet to come — as Paul has already stated. (Eph. 4:13).

But the salvation message, grace not works, remains as the very essence of Christian belief. This is the one nucleus around which authentic Christian fellowship can cluster. We may, or may not, share other like beliefs and/or interpretations of the Scriptures with others, but if this one imperative exists we can grasp their hands as brothers and sisters in the general body.

The central unifying doctrine is the simple one of the exchange of our sins for His sinlessness through the cross. (2 Cor. 5:19-21). The righteousness that is put upon us by grace through our faith in the revelation makes us one because we are all accepted by the Father as "in the Beloved". (Eph. 1:6). The atonement images its truth in many ways, as an example (1 Pet. 2.21), a victory over the powers of darkness (Col. 2:13-15), a sacrifice and expiation of sins that enables our adoption into God's family (1 Pet.2:24), and a reconciliation between God and man (2 Cor. 5:19-21). But its greatest meaning for us stands as the settlement for our sins which enables us to be accepted before God, and as those now forgiven and possessing eternal life. (Morris, 1965:402-419).

4. FOCUS ON THE FAMILY

The phrase "one baptism" (Eph.4:5) is regarded by most scholars as referring to the spiritual rebirth of the individual by the agency of the Holy Spirit which places the believing one into Christ's general body. The same figure is also used to describe the incorporating work of the Spirit in 1 Cor. 12:13. As those who interpret this phrase as referring to water baptism speak of the outward witness which confesses such an inner reality no great difference exists between the two ideas.

Most probably the idea of baptism by the Spirit into the

general body, and of its expression in water as marking a local, visible identity with Christ and His church, meld together in Paul's use of the term. Virtually all commentators from many different communions agree that the only water baptism Paul knew and practiced was the immersion of those who thus confessed that they had first placed their faith in Christ. Romans 6: 3-5 suggests immersion as it speaks of baptism as a burial. Only dead men are buried, and believers are symbolically thus treated because we are regarded as those who consider ourselves dead to sin through identification with the substitution He has offered. (Rom. 6:11).

Water baptism is a visible declaration that a believer is incorporated into the eternal fellowship of the body of Christ by the Holy Spirit. It therefore presents him or her as a valid candidate for fellowship in the earthly Christian assembly, and its meaning centers on that expression. The outward form of water baptism only united the candidates with the local gathered community of believers because it symbolized and signified their common inward reality of one Lord and one faith in Him as savior.

"One God and Father of (us) all" (Eph.4:6a) again emphasizes the focus on the family. Children of the same parent ought to be able to walk and work together in an authentic oneness of spirit and to be prepared to give and take in order to foster that family unity. Real fellowship with others in the family depends on the affective commonalities of our salvation experience not on the cognitive uniformities of our detailed understandings.

As we are children of the heavenly Father, and born of His Holy Spirit, Peter affirms we actually share His divine nature! (2 Pet. 1:4). The unifying phrases used by Paul to describe our oneness list our shared relationships to His sovereignty (over all), His purpose (through all), and His pervasive indwelling (and in all). (Eph. 4: 6b).

INDEPENDENCE AND INTERDEPENDENCE

While the New Testament tells us of the association of churches together in order to help each other with spiritual and practical needs the increasing multiplicity of denominations of Christians appears to be far from the New Testament ideal.

Paul travelled with the offerings of some churches to others, he wrote to Rome and Thessalonica from Corinth, to Corinth and Galatia from Ephesus, and from Rome he addressed the Philippians, the Colossians, and the Ephesians. Peter wrote to strangers scattered abroad throughout the whole Mediterranean region and John wrote to Christians other than those located where he ministered. Thus the basic concepts of mutual care and interdependence persistently appear in the early churches.

But biblical models of such co-operation stand firmly alongside the cherished rights of local church autonomy. While we do share our belief in individual salvation by grace with many others the self-governing independence of the local Christian assembly, the priesthood of all believers and their need for mutual ministry find a unique emphasis within our ranks. Our associations, conventions (and all other Baptist general bodies) remain advisory groups only whose whole power upon us is only one of voluntarily accepted spiritual leadership, and is never legal or directive.

When George W. Truett spoke on "Baptists and Religious Liberty" (from the steps of the national Capitol in Washington. D.C. in May, 1920) he discussed America's influences on Western civilization. He claimed that our convictions about religious liberty were the supreme contribution of the new world to the old. And he documented this to be pre-eminently a Baptist contribution. (Truett, 1950: 86). He also listed the right of private judgement and the responsibility of the individual to give account of himself to God, the absolute Lordship of Christ, and the supreme authority of the Scriptures as the only rule for Christian faith and practice as other key principles which foundation our denominational associations.

Because I share the interpretations of biblical doctrine capsuled so well in the *Baptist Faith and Message Statement (1963)* I will naturally desire to fellowship best with those who respond as I do to such matters. As I find this to be an acceptable summary of my understandings of the Scriptures I commit myself primarily to an open Christian association with those visible members of the eternal general body of Christ who share such convictions with me.

But this Baptist "confession" says nothing about the ministry of "elders", or the nature of the ministry of women, or millennialism, or any one of the many other interpretations about which Baptists have differed down through the years.

I have found a point of rest in eschatology in the position which is often described as Historic Premillennialism (or Moderate Futurism) so well summarized recently by Southern Baptist theologian Dr. John P. Newport. (1985: 103-112) This volume on Revelation now available I find to be one of the best available and his perspectives ally with those of well-known scholars such as G.R. Beasley-Murray, F. F. Bruce, E. F. Harrison, G. E. Ladd, W. S. LaSor, Leon Morris, Robert Mounce, Merrill Tenney, and many others. (Newport, 1985, bibliography, pp. 369-371.)

Perhaps it is just as well that Southern Baptists have not sought to lock down one specific interpretation of millennialism in the past. The contemporary emphases of an extreme futurism and/or dispensationalism by some on the right in Baptist theology today do not match those of the previous conservatives so many of them prize. George W. Truett taught a strong postmillenialism while pastor of First Baptist Church of Dallas, Texas. This was so pervasive that, when W. A. Criswell was proposed as his successor great concern was expressed as to whether a premillenialist could possibly preach the gospel! B. H. Carroll founded Southwestern Baptist Theological Seminary (Fort Worth, Texas) on the same postmillennial basis avowing that social reform as well as evangelism and missions would bring in the Kingdom! (Newport, 1985: 91).

Baptists have always held to a reasonable liberty in such peripheral areas. In other words we recognize that a *total* doctrinal identity among us is neither possible nor practical. As a member of Christ's general body my primary loyalty is to those who share the newness of life which I possess. I may be more comfortably able to worship, fellowship, serve and co-operate among those whose detail interpretations ally most with mine in the local church. But at the other end of the scale I can also work well with others in evangelism where the focus is on the Person and Work of Christ for salvation. As an evangelical Christian I remain dogmatic about the deity of Christ and the divine approval of His substitutionary atonement through the resurrection to secure my justification by faith. Despite other differences I shall be able to fellowship with any and all who share an authentic place in the family with me.

The Bible teaches both separation and fellowship but separation can be carried to such extremes that we fail to impact a world in desperate need of evangelization. Denominational associations are groupings of churches and individuals who unite so that they can function best to achieve the common purposes of missions and evangelism and their related tasks. Those who censure some for co-operating with others within the denomination whose doctrines do not exactly parallel their own will also have to censure Jesus. He, Himself, clearly expressed His disagreement with the pride of the Pharisees and the doctrines of the Sadducees but He joined them for worship in the Temple. He and His family participated in all the Jewish feasts and synagogue programs, and delivered many of His important teachings in them. His co-operation did not imply a full endorsement of all that others who so co-operated believed.

Paul also believed that co-operation does not require compromise and gladly worked with others who did not hold exactly what he held. He preached in the Temple and the synagogue. His inclusivist disposition is clearly indicated by his circumcision of Timothy before taking him on his missionary journey because of the Jews who might have objected to the ministry of an uncircumcised teacher in their midst. This was after the conference where the leaders of all the churches had waived this requirement! (Acts 15:5) It appears that Paul was divinely guided to be flexible in this matter.

Likewise during his last Jerusalem visit Paul yielded his freedom to do as God led without subservience to the law by agreeing to submit to a ceremonial purification. He bound himself to a formal vow in order to avoid offending these Jerusalem church leaders. (Acts 21:17-26) He was willing to co-operate for the ends of speeding the Gospel, even to the point of sacrificing personal preferences.

> For though I am free from all men I have made
> myself a slave to all, that I might win the more.
> And to the Jews I became as a Jew, that I might
> win Jews: to those who are under the Law, as
> under the Law, though not being myself under the
> Law, that I might win those who are under the
> Law; to those who are without law as without

law, though not being without the law of God
but, but under the law of Christ, that I might win
those who are without law. To the weak I became
weak, that I might win the weak: I have become
all things to all men that I may by all means save
some. (1 Cor. 9:19-22).

The only explanation for this co-operative accommodation with others was for his purpose of winning others more effectively.

DIFFERING LEVELS OF CO-OPERATION

While my fellowship will be easiest and closest therefore with those who agree with me in general Baptist areas and in detailed personal preferences of interpretation I do not need a total identity with them in all matters to relate as part of God's family. Where others do not see exactly as I do I may steadfastly affirm my convictions and seek to win others to them, but just as adamantly defend their own rights of liberty in the Lord. I believe I am bound with my fellow believers by many ties other than those of uniformity.

My doctrinal boundaries, then, can differ with the levels of co-operation needed. The Baptist denominational association, convention, agency, or other co-operative state or national body falls clearly between these two levels of local church fellowship and the trans-denominational linkage of a United Evangelistic Crusade. Seldom can Baptists be forced into a denominational co-operation which demands the same intimate detail of belief as might be needed for ease in a local church. Yet in our denominational associations we shall always require something more in common than a simple union with others who share only the experience of salvation by grace with us.

In addition to United Evangelistic Crusades Baptists often are expected to serve with other Christians to meet community needs, and serve in fraternal ministerial alliances etc. I have found that all such associations can be treated on their own merits. Sometimes the basis of association is purely altruistic and it can be treated as such. Where spiritual issues are at therefore it may sometimes be necessary for us to lay down some boundaries for participation and such bodies usually remain sensitive to the individual needs of those who work with them.

I am also continually surprised to find unexpected other authentic members of Christ's body within such groupings. One may energetically resist the many unscriptural teachings of Catholicism yet be continually delighted by the reality of a wholesome trust in Christ by an individual Catholic.

Because Christians differ in the detail interpretations of Scriptural teaching the full New Testament totality of union seems impractical today. But we may still gather with Christians of a like faith and order without negating our insight into the nature of the general body of Christ. It is right therefore for Baptists to have a separate and distinctive denominational life in order to preserve and propagate their distinctive faith. The difference between Baptists and others is not water, or sentiment. Our principles automatically separate us from other Christians. But where the clear purpose of exalting Jesus Christ as Lord and Savior only as a focus for some particular program (such as in a Graham Evangelistic Crusade) arises, Baptists (with others who are willing to put aside differences to win the lost) can co-operate harmoniously. They can also co-operate with other men and women of goodwill of any faith, or none, in altruistic endeavors, community tasks, and the like where theological distinctives are not compromised or challenged. But an organizational affiliation with national and international church councils poses some special concerns where an official continuity of such fellowship is proposed.

As each church operates as an entirely autonomous body at the local Baptist Association, State Baptist Convention, and National Baptist Convention levels such denominational connections are always one of a voluntary relationship where the organization has no actual controlling power.

Each church sends "messengers" who work with others at the common tasks of Christian education, evangelism, home and overseas missions, etc. in a purely voluntary manner. Thus the denomination has no power to direct any such affiliations, nor even to legislate any binding decisions upon any individual church or member.

Direct affiliation by a Baptist denomination as such with a controlling ecumenical body is therefore legally impossible as only each local congregation can make such an independent decision for itself. But our evangelical openness to others for fellowship also does means an willingness to share with them in organized ecumenical contexts for some very critical theological reasons.

The bulk of the constituents of those connected with national and international church councils hold ideas of a sacerdotal ministry contrary to the Baptist ideals of the priesthood of all believers. They function in worship with almost no regard for the competency of the individual soul to relate directly to God through faith, and often follow an authoritarian organizational structure which negates the functional autonomy of the local church.

The majority of the ecumenically-minded hold to a sacramental concept of salvation rather than to the biblical teachings of regeneration by grace through faith. They advocate a baptism of infants, although their own scholars agree that the New Testament practice was the immersion of believers. A large number also either favor or participate to some degree in unions of church and state.

If Southern Baptists affiliated with such groups they would be compelled to abandon their rights to interpret the truths of the Scriptures as they believe them to be. Such a surrender of their responsibility to obey the will of the Christ as they understand it would seem for them to be a denial of His Lordship. The only conscionable alternative would be to battle perpetually in an unproductive struggle over such issues within such an organization — a pointless exercise for all concerned.

4. The Categorical Imperative

When Immanuel Kant developed his pioneering studies in philosophy he divided the motivators which nourish human ethical behavior into two classes. Those which motivate action from potential benefits to be received he termed "hypothetical imperatives" (ones to which we respond subjectively, and for ourselves). Those which move us to action objectively (because their own essential rightness and goodness demands this) he termed "categorical imperatives".

We respond to the first group because of self benefit. But other and higher values motivate us from the second group. We respond to these because of intrinsic convictions that move us to fulfill their demands, even at great cost to ourselves. Thus an individual may lay down his life for another sacrificing his own self interest motivated by love, duty, or just the overpowering sense of "rightness" in such an act.

A right view of the Person and Work of Christ is the categorical imperative of Christian doctrine; "Categorical" meaning absolute, positive, and unqualified; "Imperative" meaning basic, authoritative and necessary. Faith in this reality links us to the one central, morally-essential truth which bonds us to the supreme good inherent in the almighty God. It capsules the whole biblical revelation and forms an objective dynamic which unifies us with the whole body of Christ.

5. CENTRALITY NOT IDENTITY

The *doctrinal identity* some appear to seek demands that we share a complete and absolute exactness of belief with others without the slightest measure of diversity in any opinion or interpretation. But a *doctrinal centrality* means that we fix our focus on a principal position. It means that we may choose a doctrinal axis around which all else revolves and from which all other parts can relate to each other. Only a right view of the Person and Work of Christ creates just such a doctrinal centrality.

In a real sense this is the one special commonality essential for vital Christian association. To receive another as being also within God's family each of us must see our common standing in Christ as the required integrating factor which makes us part of His general body. We may differ in many other beliefs, but this core remains as the one primary absolute, indispensable focus for the creation of any authentic spiritual fellowship.

We do not need a variety of such "fundamentals" to hold such oneness as a right view of the Person and Work of Christ is "bi-partite". One the one side the need for a perfectly sinless life to be laid down to atone for sin demands our acceptance of His deity. On the other side, because the resurrection certified His Father's acceptance of the atonement offered, we must also confess our faith in the reality of His atonement.

Only such a focus can function as the one integrating doctrinal dynamic around which the other ties of our spiritual unity and familial affinity can cluster to bind us together in mutual fellowship. This common doctrinal bond is sufficient to bring us into God's family, yet broad enough to allow for acceptable levels of individuality to persist. We may wish to define other specific interpretations of the Scriptures which facilitate denominational and other voluntary spiritual associations but we dare not let them cloud the primary doctrinal tie of a right focus on Christ's Person and Work that binds us together in Him.

The evangelical hymn *Amazing Grace* by Church of England author, John Newton (1725-1807), remains a favorite of many today because it expresses the joy of forgiveness found through faith in Christ.

Newton created 283 hymn texts, all originally in simple verse without musical settings. Among the many now forgotten in his original 1781 "Olney Hymns" collection is one he entitled — *What Think Ye of Christ?*

His mood is contemplative, and the words devotional more than exhortative. But Newton's verses center on the necessity for a clear focus on Christ as the basic doctrinal fundamental essential for Christian reality. He shows us how such a centrality illumines all faith experience and nourishes assurance. Such an axis can be the only firm nucleus around which any viable Christian fellowship must revolve.

What Think Ye Of Christ?

1. What think ye of Christ? is the test
*   To try both your state and your scheme;*
You cannot be right in the rest,
*   Unless you think rightly of Him.*
As Jesus appears in your view,
*   As He is beloved or not;*
So God is disposed to you,
*   And mercy or wrath are your lot.*

2. Some take Him a creature to be
   A man, or an angel at most;
Sure these have not feelings like me,
   Nor know themselves wretched or lost:
So guilty, so helpless am I
   I durst not confide in His blood,
Nor on His protection rely,
   Unless I were sure He is God.

3. Some call Him a Savior, in word
   But mix their own works with His plan;
And hope He his help will afford,
   When they have done all that they can.
If doings prove rather too light
   (And little, they own, they may fail)
They purpose to make up full weight,
   By casting His name on the scale.

4. Some style Him the pearl of great price,
   And say He's the fountain of joys;
Yet feed upon folly and vice,
   And cleave to the world and its toys:
Like Judas, the Savior they kiss,
   And, while they salute Him, betray;
Ah! What will profession like this
   Avail in His terrible day?

5. If asked, what of Jesus I think?
   'Though still my best thoughts are but poor;
I say He's my meat and my drink,
   My life, and my strength, and my store,
My Shepherd, my Husband, my Friend,
   My Savior from sin and from thrall;
My hope from beginning to end,
   My Portion, my Lord, and my All.

            (Newton, 1781:109-111)
            (Hymn # 89).

(17) This I say therefore and affirm together with the Lord, that you walk no longer just as the Gentiles also walk, in the futility of their (18) being darkened in their understanding, excluded from the life of God, because of the ignorance that is in them, because of the hardness of their heart;

(19) and they, having become callous, have given themselves over to sensuality, for the practice of every kind of impurity with greediness.

(20) But you did not learn Christ in this way,

(21) if indeed you have heard Him and have been taught in Him, just as truth is in Jesus,

(22) that, in reference to your former manner of life, you lay aside the old self, which is being corrupted in accordance with the lusts of deceit, 23) and that you be renewed in the spirit of your mind,

(24) and put on the new self, which in the likeness of God has been created in righteousness and holiness of the truth.

(25) Therefore, laying aside falsehood, speak truth, each one of you, with his neighbor, for we are members one of another.

(26) Be angry, and yet do not sin; do not let the sun go down on your ange,

(27) and do not give the devil an opportunity.

(28) Let him who steals steal no longer; but rather let him labor, performing with his own hands what is good, in order that he may have something to share with him who has need.

(29) Let no unwholesome word proceed from your mouth, but only such a word as is good for edification according to the need of the moment, that it may give grace to those who hear.

(30) And do not grieve the Holy Spirit of God, by whom you were sealed for the day of redemption.

(31) Let all bitterness and wrath and anger and clamor and slander be put away from you, along with all malice.

(32) And be kind to one another, tender-hearted, forgiving one other, just as God in Christ also has forgiven you.

— Ephesians 4

(14) And beyond all these things put on love, which is the perfect bond of unity.

— Colossians 3

❦

DYNAMIC FOUR: CONDUCT

THE BEHAVIORAL TIE — COMPATIBILITY NOT CONFORMITY

I went into the kitchen where my wife was making preserves. She had a pan of peaches peeled and cut up, and a big bowl of sugar, and emptied them both into a rass kettle, and I said "What are you doing?" She said, "I am preserving peaches." I said, "What is that?" She said, "I am fixing them so they will keep and keep sweet." The Bible says "The Lord will preserve us." Some of you old kicking, quarrelling, grumbling Christians think you are preserved, you are just pickled." "...perhaps some of us ought to quit singing about the 'Sweet-By-And-By' — until we begin to do something about the 'Nasty-Now-and Now'"

— *Evangelist Sam P. Jones*

To this point (in Ephesians 4) Paul has advocated the attitude of acceptance of diversity which commits us to unity rather than uniformity, the insight that builds on the actual affinity within God's family rather than looks for the ideal of the church as now a perfect entity, and the focus that centers on Christ rather than on identity of doctrine.

In the final section of this chapter (vv. 17-32) He now speaks of a Christian lifestyle with a conduct which is based on love. Only an authentic and intense affection of warm attachment and deep devotion to God's family can be the strongest integrating bond between believers. Love alone can be deep and dynamic enough to tie us together in co-operative fellowship when pressures to divide fall upon us with intensity.

A steadfast dedication to unity in the body is best expressed through a lifestyle that can be seen in our demeanor. Truly to love others in God's family means that I will hold an intense affection of warm attachment and deep personal devotion towards them.

This means that I shall be as tender towards other believers as Paul was —

> *...you know what kind of men we proved to be among you for your sake ...we proved to be gentle among you as a nursing mother tenderly cares for her own children. Having thus a fond affection for you we were well pleased to impart unto you not only the gospel of God but also our own lives, because you had become very dear to us. (1 Thess. 1:5, 2:7-8).*

Paul challenges them to display a quality lifestyle of actions, relationships, and words, such as befits the light in which they now walk and not the darkness from which we have been called. Only such a lifestyle of responsible Christian behavior gives outward evidence of the authentic inward posture of love.

1. FROM RAGS TO RICHES

In the light of all that Paul previously had said in Ephesians 4 about how we are to maintain the unity of the Spirit and to continue growing toward maturity in Christ he moves into practical and detailed answers. He reminds us first of the truth that we are new creations in Christ in verses 17 through 14, and applies this doctrine with his "therefore" of verse 25 listing its implications in verses 25 through 29. In verse 30 he alerts us to the indwelling of the Holy Spirit and the ease with which He may be grieved. This reality is then followed in verses 31 and 32 by a focus on the kind of Christian behavior which will ensure His continued presence.

Through such discussions Paul alerts us to the practical relevance of doctrine. The Christian cannot behave as others do in words or actions. The lifestyle of the unbeliever builds its character through personalities in the grip of darkness separated from the life of God. The inevitable end of such alienation will include an empty aimlessness of mind and insensitivity of heart, accompanied by an outlook of worthless self-seeking indulgence. (vv. 17-19).

Such persons are free to speak and act in ways indicative of the corruption of the old self. Secular life and knowledge possess little to make us nobler men and women. Science gives great impetus to human growth and achievement but does little to elevate the character and change the emptiness of the self-seeking or guide moral progress. Only true spiritual life can tame the natural selfish passions, curb our sharp tongues, guard our moral interests and upgrade our characters.

The natural human 'bias to be bad' which we call sin has permeated all human nature tainting it deeply. This does not mean that potentials for value are not also there, nor that we are incapable of good, but it does mean that along with our worthy acts that bias comes out constantly in our tongues, in our lifestyles, and in our relationships.

Education can sharpen the mind, culture can enlarge our sensitivities and refinement can make us more delicate in our virtues and vices, but our basic human nature continues always to drag us down. We live in a world where such corruption is so habitual that we must be constantly on guard against it. The absorption in fleshly passions by so many has led to larceny, bribery, embezzlement, sexual excesses, and a general licentiousness that means such corruption is evident from the lowest sections of criminal life in our society through to the highest levels of our national government. Greed and selfishness characterize the age and we are influenced by such practices of the secular so much that they too easily also become our accepted practices within the church.

But such lifestyles arise from unregenerate natures powerless to achieve victory over them. Indwelt by the strength of the Holy

Spirit of Christ all believers are called to a deliberate clothing of their conduct with disciplined behaviors that evidence newness of spiritual life as we have been taught. (vv. 20-24). This is a call to us for definite acts of disciplined decision which lay aside our old proud, competitive, hard hearted and secular lifestyles and to behave in an entirely new manner. We are to claim a renewal of our spirits, each is to adopt a fresh orientation of mind and self to a lifestyle characterized by righteousness and holiness.

This means everything false and distorted must be sacrificed for the truth. The hypocrite who says that the doctrine of a new self in Christ is true, but who relates to other members of the body in the selfish, insensitive, and fleshly ways, must purify those sinful behaviors and allow his life and lips to "speak" the truth and not to deny it by low-level living. (v. 25).

It means there is to be no dishonesty or deception in our relationships with others. We are called to be thoroughly authentic in all we say and do.

A lifestyle which continues in the ways of the old self can also break the fellowship where acceptable anger at wrongdoing is allowed to fester and corrupt. Anger in itself (if it be for a righteous cause) is not sinful, for our Lord Himself exhibited it at the hypocrisy and stubbornness of the Pharisees. (Mark 3:5). Hypocrisy seems also to be the root of His righteous wrath in the temple. (Mark 11:15-17), and in His judgement on a fig tree which proclaimed it had fruit by bearing leaves as the sign but which proved to be untrue to its profession and was therefore destroyed. (Mark 11: 12-14, 20).

But to be angry in a sinful manner is unworthy conduct from the believer. No place exists within the body for the bad-tempered and the irritable. Those who truly love are to be patient and not easily provoked. (1 Cor. 13:4,5). The apostle defined the practice of being as patient with each other as God is with to be as a major key to being of one mind together in the church. (Rom. 15:5,6). God's servants are especially called to be gentle not quarrelsome, and to be patient when wronged. (2 Tim. 2:24; Titus 3:2). And James characterizes the wise believer as a peacemaker and one who is at ease in all relationships.

> *But the wisdom from above is first pure, then*
> *peaceable, gentle, reasonable, full of mercy and*

good fruits, unwavering, without hypocrisy.
— James 3:17

Where anger smolders without being dealt with its evil can be cultivated, stored up, and its grievances nursed and nourished, until it leads to a bitterness of spirit, and to a vindictive hatred that seeks vengeance. Such wrath can too easily become a mood characteristic of the individual that sunders unity in the body. Christians must keep short accounts with each other, and settle them before the evening of every day or forget about them! (v.26).

Bitter and malignant hatred breeds where open and honest relationships are not maintained with continual freshness between believers. Paul says we can let the pressure out of our anger by acting upon it with despatch. When we nurture and feed anger it may explode and hurt because it builds destructive power while it simmers!

Likewise the underhand stealth, deceit, and artifice typified in the actions of the habitual robber can also enter into deceitful relationships within the body. Just as the sharpness, skill, and craft of the regenerated thief can be turned into productive uses by good labor so the acumen and skills of a clever believer can be honed and disciplined to share the best with others. (v.28).

Paul directs special attention to the matter of speech. A most obvious way in which a disciplined Christian's conduct should differ completely from those outside of Christ will be in its excision of all that is coarse, insensitive, and destructive. Verse 29 means that criticism, where it must be offered, should always be constructive and with a clear appeal to improve the situation by an offer to help with its reconstruction. Godly speech that builds up and does not corrupt will not be accusative, damming those who oppose, cutting and slashing at their actions and judging their motives or maligning their attitudes.

The climax of Paul's word in Ephesians four asserts that an undisciplined Christian life hurts the indwelling Spirit of God! (v.30). He removes His sweet influences from situations where such behaviors develop. Accordingly our peace and joy often become replaced by emotional tension, spiritual coldness and division. For the believer wrong living in any shape or form is always a fist in the face of God. The tender relationship between the Lord and His own is one of love — and love can be easily hurt. He is bruised and distressed by our careless speech. Our insensitivity in relationships with others who are in His body and our low-level living hurts and grieves Him.

In vv.31-32 Paul turns from the inward postures that are evil and destructive to some of the actual external behaviors which express them such as bitterness (settled and simmering wrath) and anger (outbursts of temper), which give rise to actions such as clamor (shouting) and slander (abusive words). His use of the word "malice" seems to be sum all the previous terms, a description of an hostile attitude that leads us to attack and work to hurt and cause the downfall of others. The way to express our love for the Lord who indwells us lies in the deliberate decision to put away all verbal railing and badness of disposition within His body, and to discipline ourselves to be tenderly forgiving.

Accordingly our discipline must include control over the tongue, the temperament, and the truth, and lead to a tender hearted forgiveness. These are the elements which form the behavioral tie of conduct that bonds us together in co-operative fellowship through Christ. But the unloving conditions and unworthy actions which Paul has listed appear too often among us. We too easily tend to bitterness against those who oppose us and too readily descend to the corrupting and the unwholesome in our communications about them. We often speak glibly of the need of forgiveness, but our hard-hearted angers too often store up hurts and brood over them so that their evil destroys that tenderness of love for other members of the body which should preserve our unity.

2. AUTHORITARIANISM

Persons who become distressed when others refuse to conform to their expected patterns of belief and action may be revealing the authoritarian roots of their own personality.

In 1950 Adorno conducted primary research into the radical social behavior of anti-Semetics and from this he isolated factors which he believed identified "the authoritarian personality". His data (gleaned from extensive personal interviews) suggested that such distorted behaviors arose mainly from early childhood experiences of frustration and their associated distorted family contexts. (Adorno, 1950).

Later researchers replaced this limited approach, (which was largely based on Freudian psychoanalytic principles) with some more holistic understandings. Contemporary authorities now see the distortions evident in an authoritarian personality as products arising from the totality of social situations experienced in all of life while the person is maturing. (Christie and Jahoda, 1954).

Some experimenters have demonstrated that authoritarians seem to be less trustworthy than others in interpersonal exchanges, and also that they prefer directive and autocratic leadership styles even when in small groups. They also appear to respond poorly to logical persuasive appeals based on information but conform well to group social norms and influences.

While authoritarians are not necessarily to be expected more in the conservative than in the liberal sectors of any issue, they can exist in equal strength on either side, appeals based upon conspiratorial themes appear to arouse their anger easiest. (This may be noted in the behaviors of extremist political groups and among those on both sides of the issue of fluoridation). (*International Encyclopedia of Psychiatry*... Vol.9, 1977:240).

EXTREMISM

The personality which many would describe as "extremist" is one whose authoritarianism regularly leads him or her to positions and behaviors which express an excessive deviation from the normal. It is applied to a group of characteristics present within one individual in such a measure that they mark a radical departure from attitudes expected from the normally mature personality.

In such a situation the inner assumptions of the extremist filter reality so as to provide unconscious distortions which affect emotional, verbal, and physical behaviors.

Because no one attitude or posture alone defines this excessive pattern no simple and specific test for its presence can be devised. Any of the following qualities may mark a tendency towards extremism. However we must never assume that the occasional presence of one or two of the below-listed perspectives verifies a particular individual as grossly abnormal.

Potential extremism can be revealed by the following

characteristic behaviors which often reveal the subconscious assumptions undergirding them.

3. SUBCONSCIOUS ATTITUDES AND CHARACTERISTIC BEHAVIORS

Subconscious Attitude # 1:

Threatened By Change

Characteristic Behaviors:

a) The unfamiliar and the unknown provokes discomfort and anxiety because of insecurity about success in the new way. Departures from the normal are therefore to be opposed because "We've never done it like that before!"
b) Impatience with slow progress toward desired goals can lead to the insistence that steps and stages of natural development bypassed and raw power be used to effect the required changes without waiting for participants to grasp why they are needed in order to then move by consensus.

Subconscious Attitude # 2:

Suspicious of The Motives of Others

Characteristic Behaviors:

a) Attacks persons rather than encourages balanced and objective discussions of issues. Spreads rumors about persons or groups which assassinate their character and destroy their usefulness.
b) Cannot take statements of the opposition at face value or accept their words as sincere.
c) Corrects others constantly their use of terms and concepts and challenges their understandings and explanations.

Subconscious Attitude # 3:

Rates Principles Above Details

Characteristic Behaviors:

Offers slogans and abstract ideas which largely ignore problems of implementation.

Subconscious Attitude # 4:

Seeks Simplistic Solutions For Complex Problems

Characteristic Behaviors:

Interprets all events according to own theories without considering alternates at all. Remains convinced that matters thought inconsequential by others possess a vast significance and importance which he or she alone can grasp correctly. Often displays a great frustration when asked to discuss practical implications of ideas.

Subconscious Attitude # 5:

Regards Any Co-operating Operation As Compromise

Characteristic Behaviors:

a) Taking a moderating position is normally viewed as aiding the enemy, never as a sensible or practical adjustment to the situation of our human condition. Choices must always be between the absolutely right and the absolutely wrong.
b) There can be no "both-and"; so each situation demands an "either-or" approach.

Subconscious Attitude # 6:

Believes Ends May Justify the Use of Any Means Available.

Characteristic Behaviors:

Uses half truths, innuendos, manipulation and guilt by association. Appeals to prejudice, fears, greed, and guilt. Employs quotations out of context. Habitually labels those who oppose with derogatory terms and is often unaware of any or all of the above behaviors in himself or herself.

Subconscious Attitude # 7:

Distrusts the Democratic Process

Characteristic Behaviors:

May pay lip service to such ideas and principles when the group decisions remain as preferred, but is unwilling to abide by the choices of the majority where these do not exactly match personal preferences. Often organizes and manipulates votes by nourishing fear. Often so acts without feeling any conscious malice or ethical stress.

Subconscious Attitude # 6:

Literal, Iconoclastic, and Single Minded

Characteristic Behaviors:

Holds little room for the artistic, the mystical or creative. Tears down established structures well but protests their errors without authentically facing the need to create suitable replacements that will actually function more effectively. The constant attempt to define one formula which, when imposed on others, is supposed to deal magically with every problem, can become obsessively compulsive.

OBJECTIVITY

Many of us read such a list as the above and respond with, "I believe I know some folks like that", and then follow this with the comment, *"They are on the side of those opposing me!"* Few among us can be objective enough to see either ourselves, or our own, in such a category. Yet each of us possesses a potential to think or act in some such excessively intense or immoderate manner. Infrequent lapses into such conduct may therefore be expected occasionally from almost all.

A major difficulty lies in how we readily discern such patterns in the behavior of others, and how blind we can be to them in ourselves. This may often be because the admission of such distortions can constitute an ego threat to the individual. But the truly mature person will receive feedback from others about his or her behaviors and seek to evaluate these with objectivity.

Students habitually charge faculty with "absent-mindedness". The real truth is that many academics run sets of back-up programs of analysis, creativity, long-range planning and other preparation to which their minds automatically revert whenever regular and repeated tasks become routine. I have learned that, when I am so engaged while walking on campus, I may neglect the expected courtesies of familial greeting. This neglect will regularly be read by others as revealing an uncaring attitude.

As I really like persons I highly value human relationships. I therefore know that I must alert myself to appear on the outside as I truly am on the inside. Unless I deliberately will to express my inward feelings of friendship by disciplining myself to look for others, and greet them as I walk, they will see me as uncaring.

It matters little what I understand my true inner attitudes to be. But it matters much what others perceive them to be through my actions. My discipline is to create an identity between those valuable inner postures and the conduct which reveals them as others have no means of identifying my attitudes except through my words, and actions.

Similarly it is pointless to explain bad behavior by the comment, "But I am not really like that!" when others reflect their awareness of conduct which suggests extremist postures. The mature individual will accept the dissonance and adjust the outward lifestyle to match the inner values. The KJV of Proverbs 11:14 advises that "in a multitude of counselors there is wisdom". In contemporary translations "wisdom" is better rendered as "deliverance" or "victory". In other words the one who is open to hear input from a variety of others and willing to adjust his or her behaviors accordingly can truly display the kind of conduct that facilitates unity.

MATURITY AND ANGER

An acid test of maturity is the willingness to accept others without being threatened by their differences to ourselves.

The person who is secure in his or her own convictions will defend them with enthusiasm but remain calm when others refuse to change. Unless a major principle of truth or ethics is compromised such a person will most often resolve any severe tension by co-operative sacrifice, or even by withdrawal, and not by aggression. But the immature are angered by views which counteract their own. The expulsion or conversion of opponents can become an obsession with them.

I sit in a chair from which I type these lines with implicit confidence that the chair will support me. But chairs have been known to collapse, and as soon as someone suggests to me that this chair may be weak I may become anxious and examine it with nervous concern. I normally ignore the truth that chairs can weaken through use and sit in absolute faith discounting any possibility of such a discomfort. But the moment someone reminds me of that potential to weakness I feel somewhat threatened.

In a similar manner some social scientists affirm that the threats arising from opposing views affect our subconscious perceptions because we fear the potential truth which may lie within them.

Thus the one most angered by the opposition may well be the one least secure in his or her own positions. The opposing ideas may be imbalanced, distorted, and misunderstood or misapplied by our antagonists but the potential truth inherent in their positions does affect us.

MATURITY AND RESPONSIBILITY

The mature person will therefore remain unangered and will not express hostility in bad words, by malicious actions, or through unforgiveness. We can best preserve such an equilibrium in our conduct as we maintain a firm commitment to that which is real and true for us. But, while we believe it would be preferable if others felt as we do, we must also accept the fact that (from the perspectives from which others "see" what they do) they hold their own positions as true for them as ours are for ourselves. We can assist them to change best by a mature and balanced attempt to reason them through to a fresh perspective.

Our own responsibility to fulfill the viable Christian lifestyle advocated by the Apostle in Ephesians 4: 17-32 is never voided by the bad behavior of others.

Paul insists that the Christian who follows his admonition to be diligent to preserve the unity of the Spirit in the bond of peace must fulfill a lifestyle of responsible verbal and relational discipline. An irresponsible lifestyle will always grieve the Holy Spirit (as he asserts in verse 30). We can never justify the employment of our own unspiritual behavior in words and deeds just because those who oppose us have first adopted such poor practices themselves.

The often quoted KJV of Amos 3:3 is sometimes falsely used to suggest that a total agreement is essential for two to walk together but the literal translation is rather "Do two men walk together unless they have made an appointment"? (N.A.S.B.). Such an association functions where two agree to meet at a certain point and accompany each other to a mutually desirable destination. Co-operative fellowship well fits such a definition because its primary need is for simple agreement to journey toward a common purpose and not necessarily for a total identity in all things.

The climactic practice which the Lord hates, according to

Proverbs 6 is the "one who spreads strife among brethren". (v.19). Unfortunately it only needs one to begin such aggressive behavior for it to multiply among others. An old farmer was walking down a country road carrying his pitchfork over his shoulder when he met another man accompanied by a fierce pit-bulldog. The dog suddenly and viciously attacked him. The farmer quietly took his long-baled pitchfork from his shoulder and expertly killed the fierce dog pinning him through to the ground. "What do you mean by injuring my dog," screamed the angry owner, "Why didn't you hit him with the other end of that pitchfork?" "Well", said the farmer, "Why didn't your bulldog come at me with *his* other end?"

Now is the time for us to place a moratorium on verbal attacks upon those who oppose us if for no other reason than that such diatribes provoke equivalent reactions.

When 1985 Southern Baptist President Charles M. Stanley addressed a divided convention in that year I believe he meant for his words to continue to be as relevant for "conservatives" as they are for "moderates". The disciplines of which he speaks are needed on all sides and they echo Paul's Ephesian words succinctly.

> *The healing must grow out of a willingness to forgive as Jesus Christ forgave, accompanied by a commitment to love other persons and to show a spirit of humility ...I believe God will do something fantastically great among Southern Baptists, if somehow you and I can take a step forward in this convention in expressing forgiveness, love, and humility to one another. Love, forgiveness, and humility aren't feelings we have but commitments we must make. How can you stand in pulpits Sunday after Sunday and expound on God's love and forgiveness if those qualities don't prevail in your heart?" (Stanley, 1985).*

The anger and bitterness among us cannot further God's will. Paul, in 1. Cor 13, insists that all truth, all sacrifice is useless without love. God may use the person who lacks a complete understanding of right doctrine, if his or her spirit is right and the focus is on Jesus Christ. But the word says that the one whose doctrine is impeccable will always minister superficially if the spirit in which the service is rendered is not one of love. The vacuum created by love's absence draws in pride, envy and selfishness.

4. COMPATIBILITY NOT CONFORMITY

We do not need conformity to a shared body of belief so much as we desperately need compatibility with a common spirit of behavior. We are called to actualize our capacity to harmonize with others who truly are our brothers and sisters in Christ and to agree that we can disagree in some areas without having to be disagreeable. Compatibility is a characteristic of Christian conduct arising from maturity and discipline. It is motivated by an inner commitment to unity rather than by convictions expressed as an outward pressure which seeks to force others to conform to our expectations.

Sometimes the right attitude is best expressed by those closest to the local church ministry. I have seen no finer words in recent years than those written by a pastor to his people in his weekly church newsletter when his own State Convention was threatened by such potential division.

> *There may be corrections that need to be made in our agencies and institutions but there is a right way to make them. Power struggle, name-calling, unChristian attitudes, bitterness, hatred, and manipulation are not the spirit of Christ. ... It is not enough to be right; we must be right with the right spirit and in the love of Christ. We must be strong in conviction, but we must also be respectful of others in their convictions. ... Frankly I don't want to be told what I have to believe, but I am willing to discuss what I believe over an open Bible, and when that discussion takes place, I want love, openness and a consideration of all the facts and all the Scriptures - not just a few isolated ones. ... I am not so interested in everyone believing as I do, but I am*

interested in us loving Christ, giving Him our best, loving one another, building His church, and being concerned for a lost and dying world. ... If we all want the truth, if we want what is best for our denomination, and if we want to exalt the Lord Jesus, it seems to me if we have been born of His Spirit we can give and take, forgive and restore, correct, and reprove, and do all in the mind of Christ. (Harris, 1987: 1,3).

This approach will require discipline, persistence, and grace. But it can be achieved by men and women of authentic goodwill.

Church of God here take your stand!
    Build His Body as He planned.
One in heart-felt sympathy,
    Fellowship and unity;
Fitly-framed and well supplied,
    By each other fortified.

Pastors, teachers, help us be
    Saints, equipped for ministry,
Not, as children, tossed about
    By the tearing winds of doubt,
But by Word and worship led,
    Growing firm in Christ our Head.

Gracious Father, Lord above,
    Give us speech of truth and love,
Choosing words that lift and bless,
    Conq'ring strife and easing stress;
Building joy and harmony,
    Reaching for maturity.

Holy Spirit, faithful guide,
    Choose the gifts that You decide
Help us best to live and grow,
    While we serve the Church below;
Make us what we ought to be —
    One, through mutual ministry. (C.S.)*

*(1988). This hymn text may be sung to the tune *Dix*.

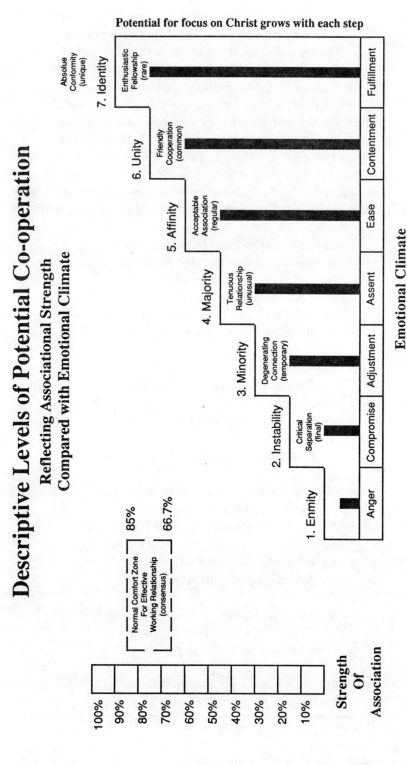

Descriptive Levels of Potential Co-operation

Reflecting Associational Strength Compared with Emotional Climate

Potential for focus on Christ grows with each step

Strength Of Association

100%
90%
80%
70%
60%
50%
40%
30%
20%
10%

85%

66.7%

Normal Comfort Zone For Effective Working Relationship (consensus)

7. Identity — Enthusiastic Fellowship (rare) — Absolue Conformity (unique)
6. Unity — Friendly Cooperation (common)
5. Affinity — Acceptable Association (regular)
4. Majority — Tenuous Relationship (unusual)
3. Minority — Degenerating Connection (temporary)
2. Instability — Critical Separation (final)
1. Enmity

Fulfillment
Contentment
Ease
Assent
Adjustment
Compromise
Anger

Emotional Climate

5. Descriptive Levels of
Co-operative Fellowship

From my over 40 years as a pastor and theological teacher I have observed that the normal "comfort zone" for co-operative fellowship is the consensus reflected when an association of individuals operates with a majority of from 66 & 2/3rds.%. to 85%. in its major decisions.

This affinity/unity consensus appears to be that which we may normally seek within the church on earth. (Many church constitutions reflect a similar conviction by their demand for such majorities for the calling of a pastor and/or other major congregational decisions.)

To achieve a continuity of absolute unanimity and 100% agreement would mean we had reached an identity which is normally impossible until we are all finally conformed to Christ in eternity. Until that time arrives we need to be content to define such a consensus as constituting sufficient an affinity and unity to enable us to function effectively while in the human condition.

I have diagrammed these and other descriptive levels of co-operative fellowship along with their comparative contexts of emotional climate, associational strength, and potential for focus on the Person and Work of Christ. (See the *frontispiece* to this volume.) It seems to me that we would profit from a greater understanding of such levels and their associated factors.

Sometimes decisive actions are possible on a slim majority, and operations can often function with difficulty even under large minority pressures. But in each case such actions are better deferred until some consensus can be reached provided it is understood that affinity and unity do not demand a total identity.

****

To this point in our reasoning we have seen that *attitude, insight, focus and conduct* are bonding factors in co-operative fellowship. We have noted that the Scriptures call for us to aim for *unity* as a purpose in the church rather than for uniformity.

Also we have recognized the reality of an authentic family *affinity* among all who constitute Christ's body rather than the expectation of an entity of sameness among them all.

Again, we have discussed how the *centrality* of a doctrinal focus on Christ and His Work on the cross is an achievable and energizing power for fellowship above the unreachable ideal of identity of belief in all matters.

We see also that a spirit of *compatibility*, worked out in speech and conduct, show this to be a practical bonding dynamic, but the attempt to make others conform is divisive.

6. THE PERFECT BOND OF LIBERTY

The above four mind-sets and lifestyles can be dynamic ties that bind. But when they are all grouped together they simply spell out the concept of love. Love is the complete bond — the essential tie. And only when the inner attitude of unity is actually executed in a program which puts that mind set of love into practice can it be affirmed as real. Only a disciplined lifestyle of love for others can truly reveal the inner posture by revealing its reality. The apostle speaks of this as the crowning tie that binds in another epistle, "And beyond all these things put on love which is the perfect bond of unity." (Colossians 3:14)

By such a comment Paul amplifies his thought from Ephesians 4:22-24 where he calls for the putting on of the new garments of righteousness suitable for a reborn person in Christ. The metaphor of "a perfect bond" imagines love as the band which girdles the whole new dress belting it around as a complete tie and bonding all together in perfect oneness.

The KJV translates "unity" in the above verse as "liberty" for love alone bonds with a perfectness that secures and completes the whole without demanding uniformity, entity, identity and conformity. We must gird ourselves securely with such a commitment if we are ever to bond together in true co-operative fellowship.

❦

PROGNOSIS

HOW DO WE GO FROM HERE?

1. DEALING WITH ELEPHANTS, MICE, AND OWLS

(A CONTEMPORARY FABLE)

No one in all the forest could stomp harder, charge faster, or trumpet louder than the mighty elephant. Not one among them all could scurry faster, search more industriously for roots and grain, nor hide more quickly and invisibly in the bushes at the slightest sign of danger than could the tiny mouse. And no one else could think more deeply, speak more cleverly, look more wisely, or stare more convincingly at others with his dark wide eyes, than could the wise old owl.

I suppose that is just as it should be because the owl held a great reputation for wisdom, and the mouse often needed to hide because the mighty elephant simply loved to stampede when he was frustrated, annoyed, and upset by others. The mighty elephant enjoyed stomping, and charging, and trumpeting so much that sometimes he stampeded just because he *was* a mighty elephant, and just because he loved to see all the fuss and the noise which he could create by so doing.

When a stampede mood was upon him the mighty elephant would crash through the forest with an enormous roar, tearing up the trees, breaking up the bushes, squashing the undergrowth with his huge heavy body, and stomping on everything his four flying feet could touch. The normal calm of the jungle echoed and re-echoed to his ear-splitting trumpet blasts of shrieking pleasure, while all the birds and animals hurried and scurried

107

helter skelter to shelter. But the elephant didn't seem to care about them at all. Stomping and stampeding seemed to him to be the very things that a mighty elephant should do and he great enjoyed the doing of them.

Unlike the mighty elephant the wise old owl sat quietly most of the time dozing on the lowest branch of the tallest oak tree in the forest. After a night of wakefulness he would dream away half the day or more reflecting on deep thoughts and vast ideas, and considering great philosophies far removed from the hum drum affairs of the everyday forest.

Most of the other animals came to him for advice about their problems. When prompted by such an eager questioner he generally would wake with a start, stare at the enquirer with his big round eyes, and nod very wisely.

After some extended thought he would then deliver a careful judgement, rather ponderously, and then drift contentedly back into his dream world confident he had delivered the very last word on the subject concerned. His counsel was always acute and perspicacious, and quite often actually helpful. All these things seemed to him to be the very things that a wise old owl should do and he greatly enjoyed the doing of them.

The tiny mouse kept busy in his daily tasks of searching for food. He shook the seeds from the tall grass, and dug among the roots of the bushes to reach their tenderized and juiciest shoots. He nibbled at the overripe fruit that fell from the forest trees, and often busied himself thus so industriously that he continued all through the day, and sometimes far into the night as well.

All these things he did seemed to be the very things that a tiny mouse should do - but he did not enjoy the doing of them - for the mouse was very afraid!

> *"Please, wise old Mr. Owl", the mouse pleaded one day, "Please tell me what I must do! The mighty elephant roars and stampedes through the forest tearing up the trees, and squashing the shrubs, and making such a terrible noise that he frightens me. His four flying feet stomp down hard on everything in sight and I am such a tiny mouse I am frightened that one day he will stomp right on me! So I scurry out of the way as fast as I can."*

"Whenever I hear him coming I shout out to warn him to be careful, but I am such a tiny mouse he never hears me, and I have such short little legs that I just can't get away quickly enough. Help me, wise old Mr. Owl, my nerves are all in pieces. What ever shall I do?"

Startled out of his dreamy dozing the old owl looked down from his perch in the lowest branch of the tallest oak tree in the forest, fixed a deep wrinkle in his brow, and adopted the most dignified posture of which he was capable. He ruffled his wing feathers so that they all stood out in iridescent splendor, widened his rotund eyes to the absolute limit of their orbicular exactness, and fixed them firmly upon his tiny enquirer. He spoke very carefully, and in the most solemn of voices.

"I fully understand your question, tiny mouse. You do well to come to me for an answer to such a problem. I perceive that you are very small and probably the mighty elephant never sees you when you rush away in fear at his trampling and his stomping. You have such a squeaky and puny little voice that it is no wonder he never hears you either."

"You must realize, tiny mouse, that elephants are not really very wicked animals, although they can be rather careless and thoughtless at times. They tend to give in far too easily to roars and rages which help them work out some of their emotions I suppose. You need to get bigger and braver than you are, and I have just the plan for you."

"When next the elephant crashes toward you change yourself into a lion - then roar as loudly as you can! Elephants fear lions. That will scare him completely away and solve your whole problem admirably!"

"What an helpful idea!" cried the tiny mouse in high glee. "Now I know why you are indeed the wisest creature in the forest. I could never have

thought of a wonderful solution like that in 1,000
years. Thank you! Thank you!"

So the tiny mouse turned back and scurried off to the forest secure in the confidence that the next time the elephant stomped and stampeded he would now have a wonderful plan to deal with him. But hardly had he travelled ten yards from the tallest oak tree in the forest when he stopped, hesitated, and then turned back with another question tumbling from his trembling lips.

"Oh wise Mr. Owl, clever Mr. Owl," he cried.
"You have really helped me so much with that
wonderful idea of turning myself into a lion when
next the elephant stomps and stampedes, and
then of roaring at him so that he goes away. But
tell me, oh wise and clever Mr. Owl, just how do
I change myself into a Lion?"

However by now the wise old owl had almost drifted back into his deep dream world and, as his big fat eyelids closed over his huge round eyes the mouse heard him mutter in a sleep-soaked voice,

"Oh, go away, tiresome tiny mouse, I am not
supposed to know everything. I have given you
the principle - now don't bother me with the
details!"

How *can* we deal with elephants, mice and owls? Some among us (moderate, conservative, and otherwise) roar and stampede about often unconscious how our stomping may hurt others as we rage. We ventilate our emotions, discharge our angers, and often feel a great deal better for our pounding about. But a great many among us, including those who least deserve to be stomped, are often crushed and flattened through this process.

Others are not prevented from being hurt because our motives may be pure. Persons can be squashed by experience whether that experience is maliciously motivated or not. Elephants who recognize how they have hurt others should repent. Like the soldiers who crucified Christ, who knew not what they did, they, too, may easily be forgiven. But if such powerful beings continue in their tirades, once they are aware of the potential havoc they may unconsciously wreak, we must confront them as firmly with their malice as Jesus confronted the Pharisees with their hypocrisy.

Too many among us are like timid mice, expecting the impossible and unwilling to face situations with courage. Many see little need for any self effort but pin their hopes to some miraculous solution magically available when needed.

But we must learn that, impotent as we may be alone, *together* we can take firmer stands and deal bravely with elephants as well as issues. Our problems will not disappear simply by scurrying away from them. We may feel small and insignificant but we must act in faith recognizing that many small voices together can reach the equivalent of a lion's roar. Opportunities for concerted action still remain the most viable avenues for the full resolution of our difficulties.

Professors, like owls, give themselves largely to meditation and reflection. Occasionally they do generate creative ideas which solve problems. But the temptation for the theorist is always to ignore the practical and to concentrate on principles rather than details.

The stubborn fact remains that in most situations all principles remain useless without the generation of some specific details for their effective application and implementation. Words and ideas alone always remain sterile. Only actions generate results.

Accordingly I offer the following counsels and specific applications as resources designed to facilitate some of the needed changes.

2. Ten New Commandments for Unity

1. Center Everything on Christ: When ever differences arise among believers or churches in association at the local, state, or national levels we must relate them to this centrality, and not to some fancied assumption that we must all believe exactly as each other among us does in all things.

Doctrinally we can agree to disagree without being disagreeable over any matters which do not directly impugn the impeccability of Christ's sinless deity or malign the validity of His atonement. Within such a focus the reality of His resurrection will be cardinal. This because He was raised for our justification (Rom. 1:4, 4:25; 1 Cor. 15:13, 14, 17) and this was his Father's certification of the value of the Life laid down in substitution for our sins.

Our committees, conventions and assemblies should plan to focus their activities deliberately around the exaltation of the Person and Work of Jesus Christ. Times for worship and praise in such meetings should possess a *primary* place in such schedules, and not be relegated to secondary levels. Structures, programs, and reports can then major on the dimensions in which they so glorify Him and give momentum to the message of His Gospel of Grace.

2. Strengthen the Spiritual: All church and denominational operations should function with a clear commitment to spiritual life and growth and not just organize to fulfill institutional structures and programs. We all assume this commitment to be so primary that we often feel we do not need to stress it, yet it is too easily overlooked. Just as Boaz left "handfuls on purpose" for Ruth to glean in his field so every Sunday school teacher, and every preacher, must ensure that spiritual treasures are to be found for hearers among all their proper studies of biblical content and backgrounds.

Seminary faculty, particularly, have to acquaint their students with enormous quantities of history, theology, literary criticism, exegesis, and exposition. We need to ensure that we warm hearts and feed souls along every journey which our courses complete.

Basic core curriculum courses on biblical christology, and the New Testament teaching concerning the atonement may therefore be much more essential than we before have imagined. In some quarters the tendency today seems to be to substitute some of the more contemporary expansions of theology for these instead of *first* providing such biblical basics as foundations against which such needed studies can best be interpreted.

3. Facilitate the Fellowship: The family affinity which binds all who are truly Christ's should reach out broadly to fellowship with those separated others who share the experience of being justified by faith with us. This does not mean a commitment to ecumenism, nor does it mean that all who claim some church relationship can be seen as our brothers and sisters. Our levels of fellowship will vary with differing situations just as in any kinship some relations are closer to us and some more distanced, yet they are still all recognized as being of the family. While some transdenominational associations are possible most of our enlarged fraternity will be directly with other individuals in the general Baptist body of the church in whom we recognize the reality of the indwelling Christ and as we then fellowship together in Him.

4. Build Up the Body: We must not be merely interested in becoming the biggest church in town but primarily in getting the Gospel out by all means to the most persons through all available means so that the Spirit of God may win the many and not just the few. Missions and evangelism must continue to be the heartbeat of all our programs.

We can fellowship closest with those who share our beliefs in some detail but we may also co-operate gladly with others who differ in order to minister redemptively to needy world. We should share our strengths and resources willingly and unselfishly to such ends. The nonconnectional denominational structure which holds the local church as its center is the only organizational tie that fastens our association with like others in place. All denominational relationships and conventions should exist primarily to foster local church growth and to provide channels for the most effective co-operation for all the churches to achieve Gospel ends.

5. Keep Your Cool: Where differences arise and injustices appear we must deal with them openly, honestly and sensitively. Patience, forbearance and self-control will rule out smoldering anger, spite, malice, and bad temper.

6. Tame the Tongue: The Christian concerned about unity will carefully choose the right words, the right occasions to

113

deliver them, and the right intonations with which to share them. We shall need to discipline ourselves to avoid the unwholesome words that corrupt and provoke like reactions in others, and can lead to shouting, brawling, clamor and slander. We will phrase thoughts in the ways best calculated to encourage positive responses from others and remember that words can batter and inflame our fellow members in the Lord's body just as surely as physical assaults can antagonize and injure them. We shall need to resist the urge to caricature their behaviors of others, or distort their positions.

7. Squash the Self: True Christian commitment requires a disciplined denial of the old self and the adoption of a lifestyle which rejects pride and competitiveness. Our previous walking in darkness must be replaced with a new walking in the light of fellowship with Christ and all his own. (1 John 1:6-7).

8. Watch How You Walk: The authentic desire for unity in the body of Christ will mean we shall resist the temptation to classify and judge the actions and motives of others. This will require humility, gentleness, and patience. Of course we must recognize that confidence in the trustworthiness of the Scriptures as we have them is a major criterion for co-operative fellowship and service.

But we shall also need constantly to remind ourselves that such faith in the Bible's present inspiration and power to be the authoritative instrument through which God reveals himself can arise from a variety of avenues, and that to insist that everyone arrives at this persuasion in the same manner is as unnecessary as it is impractical.

The positive attitude which seeks to preserve unity in the bond of peace will recognizes that uniformity is neither achievable nor desirable. A commitment to unity and affinity will mean we shall be able to accept diversity as the natural attribute of individuals within the family and not demand an impossible sameness about us all.

9. Lift Up Love: Most of all we shall concentrate on the outward expression of the inward commitment to love - the perfect bond that allows for a fullness of liberty. Only through the patient and disciplined exercise of a genuine affection for our brothers and sisters in Christ can we have unity in the church without demanding uniformity and foster affinity in the family without insisting on a total entity of sameness among us all.

Only love for Christ, and for each other in Christ, can help us focus on His Person and Work as the doctrinal tie of centrality without requiring a total identity in all belief. Only love can release us from the necessity of forcing others to conform and allow us to move into a compatibility of lifestyle which uplifts Christ and smooths the work of the Holy Spirit in our midst.

10. Act to Affirm these Attitudes: In the few pages which follow I suggest one critical, practical, and specific decision which I believe you can consider prayerfully. This may appear to be a small and insignificant action but it is one which each individual reading these pages can undertake, and one that could impact some situations quite incredibly.

3. Staying in the Mainstream

I see our present journey of faith as a voyage along a river which rapidly sweeps us all closer to an ultimate conformity with Christ.   Along such a journey progress proceeds best right within the mainstream. Those who travel too long and too close to the left bank can easily be trapped by the tides of popular religion or set adrift in the shallow backwaters of unbelief.

An earlier chapter showed how Universalism (the concept that all will be saved without the necessity of any personal faith) and the Unitarian churches (who reject the Trinity and see equal value in any and all religious beliefs), grew to their first great strengths in England and in New England. These movements arose from among the most open-minded of Baptists who, with other broad Congregationalists and independents, sought tolerance and freedom as absolutes above all else.

Those who, on the other hand, habitually hug the shorelines right of the mainstream face the ever present dangers of being caught in the cross-currents of extremism or stranded on the sandbanks of cynical judgementalism. Baptist history, unfortunately, is replete with stories of some who began well as champions of orthodoxy, but who ended as fanatics.

Many who hunt heresies everywhere end as those unable to fellowship with any save those who identify with every nuance of their own idiosyncratic individualisms.

Safety does not lie in some desperate attempt to steer a centrist course which refuses to acknowledge the pull of contrasting currents. For Baptists, as well as for most others, progress and safety both arise best where a total sensitivity to the flow of our history and principles remains in a constant dialogue with both the New Testament and our contemporary contexts. Fellowship, like momentum, accelerates best only as we remain firmly within the mainstream.

To acknowledge my own mainstream commitment I am mailing a signed copy of the affirmation reproduced on the next pages to the chief executive officer of my denomination.

Little is to be gained from the formation of another adversarial party to foster such views - we have enough schisms already.

But, for the cost of one inexpensive photocopy, an envelope, and a postage stamp, you, the reader, could join with many others to register perspectives rich with far reaching potentials for positive influence.

Should our denominational leadership receive just a few such statements many could be encouraged thereby. A significant number of such affirmations received could energize our fellowship considerably.

But an avalanche of such support would speak of an across-the-board awareness of the ties that bind us with an impact of great strength and clarity. Our leaders need to now how the bulk of their constituents feel about such priorities and concerns.

The affirmation on pages 118-119 lists some of the primary principles and attitudes worthy of support by the great majority of Southern Baptists so far as I am able to express them succinctly.

My prayer is that, as you close this volume, you may feel led to participate with me in such a grass roots expression of authentic concern and commitment.

Apart our voices may be so small that few will hear. But together we can be heard well.

Arise! And let the mice roar!

A
Mainstream
Affirmation

A MAINSTREAM AFFIRMATION

To: The President,

S.B.C. Executive Committee
901 N. Commerce Street, Suite # 750
Nashville, Tennessee, 37203.

I rejoice in the power of the Holy Spirit among God's people to lead them in an increasing growth and maturity through mutual ministry, but I also affirm that the Scriptures teach that our total agreement in all matters of doctrine awaits our ultimate conformity to Christ in the eternal state. I acknowledge, therefore, that a perfect identity of belief and practice among Baptists appears impossible to achieve while we remain in our human condition. I nevertheless affirm my confident belief in the reality of an essential spiritual unity present among all believers who genuinely confess that "Jesus Christ is Lord".

Accordingly I pledge myself to walk worthy of my calling as a member of Christ's body by practicing patience, accepting differences, extending forgiveness, increasing my sensitivities, and also by disciplining my tongue. I will endeavor to preserve the unity of the Spirit in the bond of peace. Above all I shall seek to put on love which is the perfect bond of liberty. I commit myself afresh to a theology which is biblical in substance, evangelistic in operation, and doctrinally firm in its position within the mainstream of historic Christianity.

In so doing I also affirm that a high view of the inspiration and authority of the Scriptures is vital for good fellowship, and gladly join hands with others who so believe realizing that this may be supported from several faith perspectives. I retain the right to hold and share my own such convictions in these and in other less significant, but nevertheless important, understandings wherein I may differ from others.

As a Baptist I believe in the independence and autonomy of all individuals and congregations and recognize their right to express faith through a variety of associations. I affirm that these should include prayer and support for denominational agencies and auxiliaries. I ask that Baptists in co-operative association everywhere focus more clearly on the unifying dynamic of the Person and Work of Christ - in particular on His deity, the effectiveness of His reconciling atonement, and the triumph over evil displayed through His resurrection. I am convinced that only through such freshened emphases can a real togetherness and commitment to missions and evangelism be energized and flourish.

Because of the above I pledge myself to support all fellowship which unites us in exalting Jesus Christ. I call upon my brothers and sisters to express their unity by joining together with me afresh firmly within such a mainstream.

Name (print) ....

Church ....

City ....**State** ....

Date ..../ ..../ ....

Signature ....

❦

Selected Bibliography

(limited to materials actually cited in the text)

Adorno, T. W. et. *al., The Authoritarian Personality* (New York, NY: Harper and Row, 1950)

Anderson, M. Dean, *Hymnic Practices and Preferences* (Nash., TN: Research Services Dept. Sunday School Board of the Southern Baptist Convention, 1988)

Archer, Gleason, L., "Alleged Errors and Discrepancies In the Original Manuscripts of the Bible" in Norman L. Geisler (ed.) *Inerrancy* (Grand Rapids, MI: Zondervan, 1979; pp. 57-82)

Armerding Carl, B., *The Old Testament and Criticism* (Grand Rapids, MI: Eerdmans, 1963).

"Billy Graham Answers His Critics" in *Look* (New York, NY: Feb.7, 1956, pp.47-51)

Boice, James, Montgomery, *Standing On the Rock* (Wheaton, ILL: Tyndale, 1984)

Bruce, F. F., "Criticism and Faith" in *Christianity Today* (Washington, DC: Nov. 21, 1959; pp. 9-12)

Christie, R. and Jahoda, M. (eds.), *Studies in the Scope and Method of The Authoritarian Personality* (Glencoe, ILL: Free Press, 1954)

Dobson, Ed., *In Search of Unity* (Nash., TN: Nelson, 1985)

Dobson, Ed., "Fundamentalism and Evangelicalism: a Comparison and a Contrast" in *Fundamentalist Journal* (Lynchburg, VA: March, 1986a, p.12)

Dobson, Ed., "Learning from Our Weaknesses" in *Fundamentalist Journal* (Lynchburg, VA: April, 1986b, p.12)

Dockery, David S., *The Doctrine of the Bible* (Nash., TN: SBC Convention Press, 1991)

Draper, James T., *Authority: the Critical Issue for Southern Baptists* (Old Tappan: Revell, NJ: 1984)

Erickson, Millard J., *Christian Theology*, (Grand Rapids, MI: Baker Book House, 1983; vol. 1)

Ewell, Walter A. (ed.) *Evangelical Dictionary of Theology* (Grand Rapids, MI.: Baker, 1984)

Flood, Robert, "Behind the Pages of Your Hymnbook" in *Moody Monthly*, (Chicago, ILL: Jan., 1987; pp. 51-52)

Garrett, James, Leo (et.al.), *Are Southern Baptists "Evangelicals"?* (Macon, GA: Mercer Univ. Press, 1983)

Gordon, Cyrus H., "Higher Criticism and Forbidden Fruit" in *Christianity Today* (Washington DC: Nov. 23, 1959; pp. 3-6)

Harris, J. Hoffman, "Editorial" in *Briarlake Baptist Beacon* (Decatur GA.: Oct. 21, 1987)

Henry, Carl, F., *God, Revelation, and Authority* (Waco, TX: Word, Vol. 4, 1979)

Hobbs, H.H., *The Baptist Faith and Message* (Nash., TN: Convention Press, 1971)

Honeycutt, Roy, L., "Biblical Authority; A Treasured Heritage!" in *Review and Expositor* (Louisville, KY: Southern Baptist Theological Seminary; fall, 1986; pp. 605-622)

Humphreys, Fisher, "The Baptist Faith and Message and the Chicago Statement on Biblical Inerrancy" in *Proceedings of the Conference on Biblical Inerrancy* (Nash., TN: Broadman, 1957; pp. 317 - 328)

The International Encyclopedia of Psychiatry, Psychology and Psychoanalysis, (New York, NY: Aesculapios Publishers Inc., 1977, Vol. 9)

Julian, John (ed.), *A Dictionary of Hymnology* (New York. NY: Dover Publ., 2nd. rev. ed., 1957)

Kitchen, K. A., *The Bible and Its Worship* (London, UK: Paternoster Press, 1977)

Kitchen, K. A., *The Ancient Orient and the New Testament* (Grand Rapids, MI: Eerdmans, 1966)

Kline, Meredith C., *The Treaty of the Great King* (Grand Rapids, MI: Eerdmans, 1963)

Ladd, G. E., *The New Testament and Criticism* (Grand Rapids, MI: Eerdmans, 1967)

Lumpkin, William, L., *Baptist Confessions of Faith* (Phil., PA: Judson Press, 1959)

Lumpkin, William L., *Baptist Foundations in the South* (Nash., TN: Broadman, 1961)

Morris, Leon, The Cross in the New Testament (Grand Rapids, MI: Eerdmans, 1965)

Morrison, James Dalton, (ed.) *Masterpieces of Religious Verse* (New York, NY: Harper Brothers, 1948. Reprint by Baker, Grand Rapids, MI: 1977)

New Encyclopedia Britannica, Micropaedia (Chicago, ILL: Encyclopedia Britannica Inc., 1986; vol 1, vol 4))

Newport, John P.,*The Lion and the Lamb* (Nash.,TN: Broadman, 1986)

Newton, John, *Olney Hymns in Three Books* (London, UK: T. Wilkins, 1781, 2nd. ed.)

Noll, Mark, A., *Between Faith and Criticism* (San Francisco, CA: Harper and Row, 1957)

Packer, J.I., *Knowing God* (Downers Grove: ILL: InterVarsity Press, 1973)

Packer, J. I., God Has Spoken (Downers Grove, ILL: InterVarsity Press, 1979)

Patterson, W. Morgan, *Baptist Successionism - A Critical View*, (privately published 1979); a reprint of the 1969 edition, Valley Forge, PA: Judson Press; available through Dr. W. Morgan Patterson, Golden Gate Baptist Seminary, Mill Valley, CA, 94941)

Pettinato, Giovanni, *The Archives of Ebla* (New York, NY: Doubleday and Co, 1981)

Proceedings Of the Conference on Biblical Inerrancy (Nash., TN: Broadman Press, 1987) — refer also to the bibliography therein.

Pinnock, Clark H., *The Scripture Principle* (San Francisco, CA: Harper and Row, 1984)

Pinnock, Clark H., See also *Proceedings...*, under Humphries, above.

Quebedeaux, Richard, The Worldly Evangelicals (San Francisco, CA: Harper and Row, 1978)

Reese, William, L. *Dictionary of Philosophy and Religion* (no city, New Jersey: Humanities Press, 1980)

Reid, W. Stanford, "Christian Faith and Biblical Criticism in

Christianity Today, (Washington, DC: May 26, 1972; pp. 1-12)

Robinson, H. Wheeler, *The Life and Faith of the Baptists* (London, UK: Kingsgate Press, 1946)

Shelley, Bruce L., *Evangelicalism in America* (Grand Rapids, MI: Eerdmans, 1967)

Shurden, Walter, B. "The Southern Baptist Synthesis: Is It Cracking?" in *Baptist History and Heritage* (Nash., TN: SBC Historical Commission, April 1981, pp.2-11)

Skinner, Craig, *Lamplighter and Son: The Forgotten Story Of Thomas Spurgeon And His Famous Father, C.H. Spurgeon* (Nash., TN: Broadman, 1984)

Stanley, Charles M., "The Presidential Address" at the 128th Annual Meeting of the Southern Baptist Convention, Dallas, Texas, June 11,1985), reported verbatim on daily news sheet.

Stott, John R., *Basic Christianity* (Grand Rapids: Eerdmans, 1958)

Tenney, Merill C., "The Limits of Biblical Criticism" in *Christianity Today*, (Washington DC: Nov. 22, 1960; pp. 5-8)

Walvoord, John R., *Jesus Christ Our Lord* (Chicago: Moody, 1964)

❦

APPENDIX

a) The Chicago Statement on Inerrancy[1]

In 1977 a group of evangelicals, academics, and other conservatives formed The International Council on Biblical Inerrancy after a year of preliminary planning. They met again in 1978, in Chicago, and drafted *The Chicago Statement On Biblical Inerrancy* which is reproduced, along with its preliminary statements, in the pages which follow.

Drs. James M. Boice, James A. Packer, Gleason L. Archer, Roger R. Nicole, Norman L. Geisler, and Carl F.H. Henry were among the better-known academics and leaders in the movement.

A decade later, in September, 1987, the Council dissolved its organization and handed over to the National Association of Evangelicals "the responsibility to uphold the authority of the Scriptures and their application to daily life". (These were the terms by which the religious press reports described their actions).

Persistent rumors abound that the group had foundered on differing interpretations of various applications of the Scriptures to life such as the ministries of women and similar theological 'hot potatoes'.

It seems possible that they realized a confession of inerrancy such as that which follows is possible, but that the more such a group gets into hermeneutics and practical interpretations and applications of the Scriptures the more difficult agreements become.

The official comment was that they had finished the task for

---

[1] Reprinted by permission of Dr. James L. Boice, and of the National Association of Evangelicals, Washington, D.C.

which they had been formed. It may therefore be unfair to judge that their disbanding was caused in large measure by such tensions.

However it is known that ten members of the original Chicago group refused to sign the 1978 inerrancy statement because of individual problems they found with its wording. Some who attended their 1982 session say that an even larger number might have refused signing their second statement (*The Chicago Statement On Hermeneutics,* 1982) had not those present agreed that *their signatures meant only their support of the tenor of the document*, and not necessarily a commitment to all of its details.

b) The Baptist Faith and Message[2]

The Inerrancy Statement which follows is not necessarily an extraordinarily comfortable one for Southern Baptists but it does allow some surprising room for many mainstream ideas. Among these perspectives is the specific confession that a belief in inerrancy is not prerequisite for salvation or effective ministry.

Some omissions which cause concern are

1. No strong statement appears asserting that the perspectives adopted arise fundamentally as a "faith position".
2. The document insists on discussing the original autographs (which no one can examine) at some length, and consequently neglects fixing a strong focus where we need it most - on the Bible as we have it today.

Nevertheless the statement has been adopted as the guideline for writers of the *New American Commentary* - a multi-volume work now well into production by Southern Baptists.[3]

---

[2] Available by request from any local Southern Baptist Church or from the Sunday School Board of the Southern Baptist Convention, 127 Ninth Ave. N., Nash., TN, 37234.

[3] Some of the writers of that commentary (not identified with hyper-fundamentalism) have confided to me that the Chicago Statement imposes no limits which embarrass their scholarship.

The new academic dean of Southern Baptist Seminary has provided a recent scholarly and conservative definition of inspiration which he calls "balanced inerrancy". This may well become the focus point for further commitment.[4]

This appears to suggest that such a position may become a unifying and workable one for most Southern Baptists.

---

[4] He discusses *Naive Inerrancy* (assuming all to be literally dictated by God), *Absolute Inerrancy* (rejecting mechanical dictation but yet still affirming absolute accuracy in all historical records and scientific perspectives), *Limited Inerrancy* (advocating that in salvation, ethics, faith, and practice biblical truth may be trusted), *Functional Inerrancy* (believing the biblical revelation can be trusted not to fail in its purpose to reveal God and bring persons into His fellowship), and the *Errant But Authoritative* position (which sees the Bible not as revelation but only as a pointer to a potential encounter with God). He sees these all as faulty and defines the *Balanced Inerrancy* view as "When all the facts are known, the Bible, in its autographs (that is the original documents) properly interpreted in light of the culture and means of communication that had developed by the time of its composition, is completely true in all that it affirms, to the degree of precision intended by the author's purpose in relation to God and His creation."(Dockery, David S., *The Doctrine of the Bible* (Nash., TN: SBC Convention Press, 1991).

Developing the discussion in chapter 6 he uses the phrase "original autographs" to apply to any translation to the degree in which it represents the original word. Because the Bible is both a human and divine product he affirms that biblical and literary tools may be employed with confidence and with faith-oriented presuppositions. *Balanced Inerrancy* is a faith position. But upon close examination all the other positions mentioned above are also found to be so as I have demonstrated previously (see my pp. 24-42).

THE CHICAGO STATEMENT ON BIBLICAL INERRANCY

The authority of Scripture is a key issue for the Christian church in this and every age. Those who profess faith in Jesus Christ as Lord and Savior are called to show the reality of their discipleship by humbly and faithfully obeying God's written Word. To stray from Scripture in faith or conduct is disloyalty to our Master. Recognition of the total truth and trustworthiness of Holy Scripture is essential to a full grasp and adequate confession of its authority.

The following Statement affirms this inerrancy of Scripture afresh, making clear our understanding of it and warning against its denial. We are persuaded that to deny it is to set aside the witness of Jesus Christ and of the Holy Spirit and to refuse that submission to the claims of God's own Word which marks true Christian faith. We see it as our timely duty to make this affirmation in the face of current lapses from the truth of inerrancy among our fellow Christians and misunderstanding of this doctrine in the world at large.

This Statement consists of three parts: a Summary Statement, Articles of Affirmation and Denial, and an accompanying Exposition. It has been prepared in the course of a three-day consultation in Chicago. Those who have signed the Summary Statement and the Articles wish to affirm their own conviction as to the inerrancy of Scripture and to encourage and challenge one another and all Christians to growing appreciation and understanding of this doctrine. We acknowledge the limitations of a document prepared in a brief, intensive conference and do

Reproduced by permission

not propose that this Statement be given creedal weight. Yet we rejoice in the deepening of our own convictions through our discussions together, and we pray that the Statement we have signed may be used to the glory of our God toward a new reformation of the church in its faith, life and mission.

We offer this Statement in a spirit, not of contention, but of humility and love, which we purpose by God's grace to maintain in any future dialogue arising out of what we have said. We gladly acknowledge that 'many who deny the inerrancy of Scripture do not display the consequences of this denial in the rest of their belief and behavior, and we are conscious that we who confess this doctrine often deny it in life by failing to bring our thoughts and deeds, our traditions and habits, into true subjection to the divine Word.

We invite response to this statement from any who see reason to amend its affirmations about Scripture by the light of Scripture itself, under whose infallible authority we stand as we speak. We claim no personal infallibility for the witness we bear, and for any help which enables us to strengthen this testimony to God's Word we shall be grateful.

A SHORT STATEMENT

1. God, who is himself truth and speaks truth only, has inspired Holy Scripture in order thereby to reveal himself to lost mankind through Jesus Christ as Creator and Lord, Redeemer and Judge. Holy Scripture is God's witness to himself.

2. Holy Scripture, being God's own Word, written by men prepared and superintended by his Spirit, is of infallible divine authority in all matters upon which it touches: it is to be believed, as God's instruction, in all that it affirms; obeyed, as God's command, in all that it requires; embraced, as God's pledge, in all that it promises.

3. The Holy Spirit, Scripture's divine author, both authenticates it to us by his inward witness and opens our minds to understand its meaning.

4. Being wholly and verbally God-given, Scripture is without error or fault in all its teaching, no less in what it states about

God's acts in creation, about the events of world history, and about its own literary origins under God, than in its witness to God's saving grace in individual lives.

5. The authority of Scripture is inescapably impaired if this total divine inerrancy is in any way limited or disregarded, or made relative to a view of math contrary to the Bible's own; and such lapses bring serious loss to both the individual and the church.

ARTICLES OF AFFIRMATION AND DENIAL

Article 1.   **We affirm** that the Holy Scriptures are to be received as the authoritative Word of God.

We deny that the Scriptures receive their authority from the church, tradition, or any other human source.

Article II.   **We affirm** that the Scriptures are the supreme written norm by which God binds the conscience, and that the authority of the church is subordinate to that of Scripture.

We deny that church creeds, councils, or declarations have authority greater than or equal to the authority of the Bible.

Article 111.   **We affirm** that the written Word in its entirety is revelation given by God.

We deny that the Bible is merely a witness to revelation, or only becomes revelation in encounter, or depends on the responses of men for its validity.

Article IV.   **We affirm** that God who made mankind in his image has used language as a means of revelation.

We deny that human language is so limited by our creatureliness that it is rendered inadequate as a vehicle for divine revelation. We further deny that the corruption of human culture and language through sin has thwarted God's work of inspiration.

Article V.   **We affirm** that God's revelation within the Holy Scriptures was progressive.

We deny that later revelation, which may fulfill earlier revelation, ever corrects or contradicts it. We further deny that any normative revelation has been given since the completion of the New Testament writings.

Article VI.   **We affirm** that the whole of Scripture and all its parts, down to the very words of the original, were given by divine inspiration.

We deny that the inspiration of Scripture can tightly be affirmed of the whole without the parts, or of some parts but not the whole.

Article VII.   **We affirm** that inspiration was the work in which God by his Spirit, through human writers, gave us his Word. The origin of Scripture is divine. The mode of divine inspiration remains largely a mystery to us.

We deny that inspiration can be reduced to human insight, or to heightened states of consciousness of any kind.

Article VIII.   **We affirm** that God in his work of inspiration utilized the distinctive personalities and literary styles of the writers whom he had chosen and prepared.

We deny that God, in causing these writers to use the very words that he chose, overrode their personalities.

Article IX. **We affirm** that inspiration, though not conferring omniscience, guaranteed true and trustworthy utterance on all matters of which the Biblical authors were moved to speak and write.

We deny that the finitude or fallenness of these writers, by necessity or otherwise, introduced distortion or falsehood into God's Word.

Article X. **We affirm** that inspiration, strictly speaking, applies only to the autographic text of Scripture, which in the providence of God can be ascertained from available manuscripts with great accuracy. We further affirm that copies and translations of Scripture are the Word of God to the extent that they faithfully represent the original.

We deny that any essential element of the Christian faith is affected by the absence of the autographs. We further deny that this absence renders the assertion of biblical inerrancy invalid or irrelevant.

Article XI. **We affirm** that Scripture, having been given by divine inspiration, is infallible, so that, far from misleading us, it is true and reliable in all the matters it addresses.

We deny that it is possible for the Bible to be at the same time infallible and errant in its assertions. Infallibility and inerrancy may be distinguished, but not separated.

Article XII.   **We affirm** that Scripture in its entirety is inerrant, being free from all falsehood, fraud, or deceit.

We deny that Biblical infallibility and inerrancy are limited to spiritual, religious, or redemptive themes, exclusive of assertions in the fields of history and science. We further deny that scientific hypotheses about earth history may properly be used to overturn the teaching of Scripture on creation and the flood.

Article XIII.   **We affirm** the propriety of using inerrancy as theological term with reference to the complete truthfulness of Scripture.

We deny that it is proper to evaluate Scripture according to standards of truth and error that are alien to its usage or purpose. We further deny that inerrancy is negated by biblical phenomena such as a lack of modern technical precision, irregularities of grammar or spelling, observational descriptions of nature, the reporting of falsehoods, the use of hyperbole and round numbers, the topical arrangement of material, variant selections of material in parallel accounts, or the use of free citations.

Article XIV.   **We affirm** the unity and internal consistency of Scripture.

We deny that alleged errors and discrepancies that have not yet been resolved vitiate the truth claims of the Bible.

Article XV.   **We affirm** that the doctrine of inerrancy is grounded in the teaching of the Bible about inspiration.

We deny that Jesus' teaching about Scripture may be dismissed by appeals to accommodation or to any natural limitation of his humanity.

Article XVI.

We affirm that the doctrine of inerrancy has been integral to the Church's faith throughout its history.

We deny that inerrancy is a doctrine invented by scholastic Protestantism, or is a reactionary position postulated in response to negative higher criticism.

Article XVII.

We affirm that the Holy Spirit bears witness to the Scriptures, assuring believers of the' truthfulness of God's written Word.

We deny that this witness of the Holy Spirit operates in isolation from or against Scripture.

Article XVIII.

We affirm that the text of Scripture is to be interpreted by grammatico-historical exegesis, taking account of its literary forms and devices, and that Scripture is to interpret Scripture.

We deny the legitimacy of any treatment of the text or quest for sources lying behind it that leads to relativizing, dehistoricizing, or discounting its teaching, or rejecting its claims to authorship.

Article XIX.

We affirm that a confession of the full authority, infallibility, and inerrancy of Scripture is vital to a sound understanding of the whole of the Christian faith. We further affirm that such confession should lead to increasing conformity to the image of Christ.

We deny that such confession is necessary for salvation. However, we further deny that inerrancy can be rejected without grave consequences, both to the individual and to the church.

EXPOSITION

Our understanding of the doctrine of inerrancy must be set in context of the broader teachings of the Scripture concerning itself. This exposition gives an account of the outline of doctrine from *which* our summary statement and articles are drawn.

CREATION, REVELATION AND INSPIRATION

The Triune God, who formed all things by his creative utterances and governs all things by his Word of decree, made mankind in his own image for a life of communion with himself, on the model of the eternal fellowship of loving communication within the Godhead. As God's image-bearer, man was to hear God's Word addressed to him and to respond in the joy of adoring obedience. Over and above God's self-disclosure in the created order and the sequence of events within it, human beings from Adam on have received verbal messages from him, either directly, as stated in Scripture, or indirectly in the form of part or all of Scripture itself.

When Adam fell, the Creator did not abandon mankind to final judgment but promised salvation and began to reveal Himself as Redeemer in a sequence of historical events centering on Abraham's family and culminating in the life, death, resurrection, present heavenly ministry, and promised return of Jesus Christ. Within this frame God has from time to time spoken specific words of judgment and mercy, promise and command, to sinful human beings so drawing them into a covenant relation of mutual commitment between him and them in which he blesses them with gifts of grace and they bless him in responsive adoration. Moses, whom God used as mediator to carry his words to His people at the time of the Exodus, stands at the head of a long line of prophets in whose mouths and writings God put his words for delivery to Israel. God's purpose in this succession of messages was to maintain his covenant by causing his people to know his Name — that is, his nature — and his will both of precept and purpose in the present and for the future. This line of prophetic spokesmen from God came to completion in Jesus Christ, God's incarnate Word, who was himself a prophet — more than a prophet, but not less — and in the apostles and prophets of the first Christian generation. When God's final and climactic message, his word to the world concerning Jesus Christ, had been spoken and elucidated by those in the apostolic circle, the sequence of revealed messages ceased. Henceforth, the church was to live and know God by what he had already said, and said for all time.

At Sinai God wrote the terms of his covenant on tables of stone, as his enduring witness and for lasting accessibility, and throughout the period of prophetic and apostolic revelation he prompted men to write the messages given to and through them, along with celebratory records of his dealings with his people, plus moral reflections on covenant life and forms of praise and prayer for covenant mercy. The theological reality of inspiration in the producing of biblical documents corresponds to that of spoken prophecies: although the human writers' personalities were expressed in what they wrote, the words were divinely constituted. Thus, what Scripture says, God says; its authority is his authority, for he is its ultimate Author, having given it through the minds and words of chosen and prepared men who in freedom and faithfulness "spoke from God as they were carried along by the Holy Spirit" (2 Peter 1:21). Holy Scripture must be acknowledged as the Word of God by virture of its divine origin.

AUTHORITY: CHRIST AND THE BIBLE

Jesus Christ, the Son of God who is the Word made flesh, our Prophet, Priest, and King, is the ultimate Mediator of God's communication to man, as he is of all God's gifts of grace. The revelation he gave was more than verbal; he revealed the Father by his presence and his deeds as well. Yet his words were crucially important; for he was God, he spoke from the Father, and his words will Judge all men at the last day.

As the prophesied Messiah, Jesus Christ is the central theme of Scripture. The Old Testament looked ahead to him; the New Testament looks back to his first coming and on to his second. Canonical Scripture is the divinely inspired and therefore normative witness to Christ. No hermeneutic, therefore, of which the historical Christ is not the focal point is acceptable. Holy Scripture must be treated as what it essentially is — the witness of the Father to the incarnate Son.

It appears that the Old Testament canon had been fixed by the time of Jesus. The New Testament canon is likewise now closed inasmuch as no new apostolic witness to the historical Christ can now be borne. No new revelation (as distinct from Spirit-given understanding of existing revelation) will be given until Christ comes again. The canon was created in principle by divine inspiration. The church's part was to discern the canon which God had created, not to devise one of its own.

The word *canon,* signifying a rule or standard, is a pointer to authority, which means the right to rule and control. Authority in Christianity belongs to God in his revelation, which means, on the one hand, Jesus Christ, the living Word, and, on the other hand, Holy Scripture, the written Word. But the authority of Christ and that of Scripture are one. As our Prophet, Christ testified that Scripture cannot be broken. As our Priest and King, he devoted his earthly life to fulfilling the law and the prophets, even dying in obedience to the words of Messianic prophecy. Thus, as he saw Scripture attesting him and his authority, so by his own submission to Scripture he attested its authority. As he bowed to his Father's instruction given in his Bible (our Old Testament), so he requires his disciples to do - not, however, in isolation but in conjunction with the apostolic witness to himself which he undertook to inspire by his gift of the Holy Spirit. 50 Christians show themselves faithful servants of their Lord by bowing to the divine instruction given in the prophetic and apostolic writings which together make up our Bible.

By authenticating each other's authority, Christ and Scripture coalesce into a single fount of authority. The Biblically-interpreted Christ and the Christ-centered, Christ-proclaiming Bible are from this standpoint one. As from the fact of inspiration we infer that what Scripture says, God says, so from the revealed relation between Jesus Christ and Scripture we may equally declare that what Scripture says, Christ says.

INFALLIBILITY, INERRANCY. INTERPRETATION

Holy Scripture, as the inspired Word of God witnessing authoritatively to Jesus Christ, may properly be called *infallible* and *inerrancy*. These negative terms have a special value, for they explicitly safeguard crucial positive truths.

Infallible signifies the quality of neither misleading nor being misled and so safeguards in categorical terms the truth that Holy Scripture is a sure, safe, and reliable rule and guide in all matters.

Similarly, *inerrant* signifies the quality of being free from all falsehood or mistake and so safeguards the truth that Holy Scripture is entirely true and trustworthy in all its assertions.

We affirm that canonical Scripture should always be interpreted on the basis that it is infallible and inerrant. However, in determining what the God-taught writer is asserting in each passage, we must pay the most careful attention to its claims and character as a human production. In inspiration, God utilized the culture and conventions of his penman's milieu, a milieu that God controls in his sovereign providence; it is misinterpretation to imagine otherwise.

So history must be treated as history, poetry as poetry, hyperbole and metaphor as hyperbole and metaphor, generalization and approximation as what they are, and so forth. Differences between literary conventions in Bible times and in ours must also be observed: since, for instance, non-chronological narration and imprecise citation were conventional and acceptable and violated no expectations in those days, we must not regard these things as faults when we find them in Bible writers. When total precision of a particular kind was not expected nor aimed at, it is no error not to have achieved it. Scripture is inerrant, not in the sense of being absolutely precise by modern standards, but in the sense of making good its claims and achieving that measure of focused truth at which its authors aimed.

The truthfulness of Scripture is not negated by the appearance in it of irregularities of grammar or spelling, phenomenal descriptions of nature, reports of false statements [e.g., the lies of Satan), or seeming discrepancies between one passage and another. It is not fight to set the so-called "phenomena" of Scripture against the teaching of Scripture about itself. Apparent inconsistencies should not be ignored. Solution of them, where this can be convincingly achieved, will encourage our faith, and where for the present no convincing solution is at hand we shall significantly honor God by trusting his assurance that his Word is true, despite these appearances, and by maintaining our confidence that one day they will be seen to have been illusions.

Inasmuch as all Scripture is the product of a single divine mind, interpretation must stay within the bounds of the analogy of Scripture and eschew hypotheses that would correct one biblical passage by another, whether in the name of progressive revelation or of the imperfect enlightenment of the inspired writer's mind.

Although Holy Scripture is nowhere culture-bound in the sense that its teaching lacks universal validity, it is sometimes culturally conditioned by the customs and conventional views of a particular period, so that the application of its principles today calls for a different sort of action.

SKEPTICISM AND CRITICISM

Since the Renaissance, and more particularly since the Enlightenment, world-views have been developed which involve skepticism about basic Christian tenets. Such are the agnosticism which denies that God is knowable, the rationalism which denies that he is incomprehensible, the idealism which denies that he is transcendent, and the existentialism which denies rationality in his relationships with us. When these un- and anti-biblical principles seep into men's theologies at a presuppositional level, as today they frequently do, faithful interpretation of Holy Scripture becomes impossible.

TRANSMISSION AND TRANSLATION

Since God has nowhere promised an inerrant transmission of Scripture, it is necessary to affirm that only the autographic text of the original documents was inspired and to maintain the need of textual criticism as a means of detecting any slips that may have crept into the text in the course of its transmission. The verdict of this science, however, is that the Hebrew and Greek text appear to be amazingly well preserved, so that we are amply justified in affirming, with the Westminster Confession, a singular providence of God in this mailer and in declaring that the authority of Scripture is in no way jeopardized by the fact that the copies we possess are not entirely error-free.

Similarly, no translation is or can be perfect, and all translations are an additional step away from the *autographa.* Yet the verdict of linguistic science is that English-speaking Christians, at least, are exceedingly well served in these days with a host of excellent translations and have no cause for hesitating to conclude that the true Word of God is within their reach. Indeed, in view of the frequent repetition in Scripture of the main matters with which it deals and also of the Holy Spirit's constant witness to and through the Word, no serious translation of Holy Scripture will so destroy its meaning as to render it unable to make its reader "wise for salvation through faith in Christ Jesus" (2 Tim. 3: 15).

INERRANCY AND AUTHORITY

In our affirmation of the authority of Scripture as involving its total truth, we are consciously standing with Christ and his apostles, indeed with the whole Bible and with the main stream of church history from the first days until very recently. We are concerned at the casual, inadvertent, and seemingly thoughtless way in which a belief of such far-reaching importance has been given up by so many in our day.

We are conscious too that great and grave confusion results from ceasing to maintain the total truth of the Bible whose authority one professes to acknowledge. The result of taking this step is that the Bible which God gave loses its authority, and what has authority instead is a Bible reduced in content according to the demands of one's critical reasonings and in principle reducible still further once one has started. This means that at bottom independent reason now has authority, as opposed to Scriptural teaching. If this is not seen and if for the time being basic evangelical doctrines are still held, persons denying the full truth of Scripture may claim an evangelical identity while methodologically they have moved away from the evangelical principle of knowledge to an unstable subjectivism, and will find it hard not to move further.

We affirm that what Scripture says, God says. May he be glorified. Amen and Amen.

ABOUT THE AUTHOR

Craig Skinner has completed formal studies at ten different colleges, universities, and graduate schools in America and overseas, and taught on the faculties of five. His advanced degrees in theology and education include two secular university doctorates. His Ph.D. (in education and social psychology) is from the State University of Queensland, Australia, where he was born and where he served for a total of twenty years as a Baptist pastor and theological school academic dean. His Dr. Theol. is from the University of South Africa. In the U.S.A. he has pastored in Chicago (A.B.C) and Atlanta (S.B.C.), and served as Professor of Practical Theology at Biola University/ Talbot Theological Seminary in Los Angeles. Since 1982 he has been Professor of Preaching at Golden Gate Baptist Theological Seminary in California, (S.B.C.).

Dr. Skinner is widely known as a conference leader and pulpit guest, and for his seminars and lectures in creative preaching and in leadership psychology. He has authored eighty-five professional projects, journal articles, and research papers which have appeared in a diversity of publications ranging from *Christianity Today, Baptist History and Heritage,* and the *Australian Evangelical, to SBC Search, Church Administration,* and *Preaching.* The best known of his four previous volumes are *The Teaching Ministry of the Pulpit* (Baker, 1973), and *Lamplighter and Son — The Forgotten Story of Thomas Spurgeon and His Famous Father, C.H. Spurgeon,* (Broadman, 1984).